D0142396

THE DECLINE AND FALL OF THE U.S. ECONOMY

THE DECLINE AND FALL OF THE U.S. ECONOMY

How Liberals and Conservatives
Both Got It Wrong

William McDonald Wallace

 PRAEGER

AN IMPRINT OF ABC-CLIO, LLC
Santa Barbara, California • Denver, Colorado • Oxford, England

Library of Congress Cataloging-in-Publication Data

Wallace, William McDonald.
   The decline and fall of the U.S. economy : how liberals and conservatives both got it wrong / William McDonald Wallace.
      p. cm.
   Includes bibliographical references and index.
      ISBN 978–0–313–38379–3 (hard copy : alk. paper) — ISBN 978–0–313–38380–9 (ebook)
1. United States—Economic policy—2001–2009. 2. Financial crises—United States.
3. Fiscal policy—United States. I. Title.
HC106.83.W55   2010
330.973—dc22   2010006051

ISBN: 978–0–313–38379–3
EISBN: 978–0–313–38380–9

14 13 12 11 10   1 2 3 4 5

This book is also available on the World Wide Web as an eBook.
Visit www.abc-clio.com for details.

Praeger
An Imprint of ABC-CLIO, LLC

ABC-CLIO, LLC
130 Cremona Drive, P.O. Box 1911
Santa Barbara, California 93116-1911

This book is printed on acid-free paper (∞)

Manufactured in the United States of America

CONTENTS

PREFACE

Two things brought down the economy in 2008. First, after 1980, came financial deregulation pushed mainly by conservatives. Second came the social engineering in housing pushed mostly by liberals. This book will look behind the scenes of ideology, theory, and policy to see how and why that 2008 crash took place.

Conservatives pushed deregulation because of their overabundant faith in the wisdom of free markets. Often called *laissez-faire*, this faith insists that the government keep its hands off the economy. And the government did indeed take its hands off, gradually deregulating the financial sector beginning about 1980 and ending with the repeal of the Glass-Steagall banking act in 1999. That repeal, along with earlier deregulation, opened the door to speculative excess, and it promptly ran wild. That excess led to untrammeled greed, to outrageous predatory lending, and to the loss of fiduciary integrity in the entire financial sector as lawyers, rating agencies, and accountants joined in to share in the swag. Those professions had long kept the folks in finance reasonably honest. But once Glass-Steagall was repealed, these professions lost much of their professional integrity. That loss was first clearly revealed by the collapse of the Enron Corporation in 2001.

After 1980, one speculative bubble followed another. The final collapse came in October of 2008 when the subprime mortgage bubble burst wide open, triggering a global collapse. About two trillion dollars in wealth vanished as the price of homes and stocks fell sharply. In addition, many "derivative" financial instruments—derived from those assets—quickly became "toxic waste" and their market value fell to zero. But the debt incurred to leverage all those bubbles remained in place to ruin millions.

The subprime mortgage bubble that wrecked the global financial sector got a big assist from the liberals. For their part, liberals had an overabundant faith in the duty of the government to provide for the disadvantaged and see to their welfare. The critical moment here was when a liberal Congress passed laws that indirectly compelled the banks to offer mortgages to the poor such that they could buy houses they could not possibly afford. This NINJA (No Income, No Job or Assets) project went by the ironic name of "affordable housing."

That term was doubly ironic. Not only did NINJA loans spark a surge in the demand for housing by the poor, as expected, it also sparked a surge in demand from highly leveraged speculators. This double surge in demand drove the price of housing so high that housing became unaffordable for all but the very rich. Those outlandish prices forced the bubble to burst in October 2008, and thereby ruin millions and bring down the global financial structure. Again, this book sorts out the complex policy interactions and the theories and ideologies behind them that produced this collapse. We will see throughout that both conservative and liberal policies and their underlying theories were behind it all.

I write this book as a newly humbled conservative. Yet, I have been a sort of maverick conservative ever since leaving graduate school. By conservative I mean that I believed strongly that free enterprise performed far better than communism, a conclusion I came to in 1947. However, when I left graduate school in 1960 to take a job as an economist at the Boeing Co., I had concluded that both the conservative classical theory and the liberal neoclassical theory of economics each had serious flaws, some of which they shared in common. Those flaws by no means pushed me toward socialism because I saw that those flaws could be corrected without hurting the free enterprise system. Indeed, correcting them would actually make the system stronger.

As I saw it early on, both theories contained grossly distorted views of labor that willfully ignored one simple fact: humans are social animals. As such, they are driven as much by emotion as by pure reason, perhaps even more. Everyday experience of life amply proves as much. Moreover, it was clear to me after my first year at Boeing that neither theory had any understanding about how innovations in technology drive economic growth. One major Austrian economist, Joseph A. Schumpeter, saw that truth, but neither classical nor neoclassical theory really incorporated his views. I also concluded that the folks in finance, whether in business or academia, aside from a few exceptions, were just plain dumb about economics. I saw why operations managers put down finance people by calling them "bean counters." Still, only in the twenty-first century did I see that the term "dumb" does not come close to describing the folks in finance when a policy of *laissez-faire* removes the previous constraints that kept them honest and allows them to freely express their dumbness.

I also learned while writing an earlier book on cultural and economic evolution[1] not only how our innovations drive economic growth, but that they do so in a process of cultural evolution that Darwin ignored. If events seriously disrupt a stable ecosystem, a chaotic new order emerges. The disruption can release the survivors of it from previous ecological constraints on their behavior. I saw boom and bust as a core process of both biological and cultural evolution. Release offers new opportunities with no constraints; a competitive rush results in overexploitation. A crash follows. Economic history is full of such boom and bust examples. That includes the Great Depression in 1929, the year of my birth, and the meltdown of 2008, the year of my retirement.

Here, let me back up a bit to 1947. In my freshman year at the College (now University) of Puget Sound in Tacoma, Washington, I took Economics 101. My professor, Dr. Charles T. Battin, described classical economics dating back to Adam Smith, and I was quickly won over. It was nice to think that people working on their own behalf to make a living would also produce socially useful outcomes for others, thanks to the division of labor and the "invisible hand" of market competition. It seemed such a free enterprise system needed no top down dictator such as Hitler or Stalin. Moreover, I was horrified by Dr. Battin's description of life in communist Russia under Stalin, even though the Cold War was still a year away.

The following June (1948) I got a job as a crewmember on the USAT *Republic*, an army transport ship operating out of Seattle that hauled troops and their civilian dependents between Seattle and Yokohama. I made two trips to Japan that summer. It took forever to unload and load transports in those days and to my delight I had little to do while in port. So my crewmates and I toured the Tokyo and Yokohama areas, taking advantage of the free train rides available to the American occupation forces. While the Japanese had cleared away much of the debris, the massive devastation caused by our B-29 bombers was still obvious. I concluded that the United States had knocked out Japan as a serious economic rival for a hundred years or more.

Two years later, in 1950 North Korea invaded South Korea. The minute I heard the news on my car radio, I knew I could become cannon fodder. As I rushed to finish my degree, my high school economics teacher, Colonel Peterkin, who commanded an army reserve unit, talked me into joining his regiment, the 415th of the 104th Timber Wolf Division, and applying for a commission. Once commissioned, I requested active duty. I received my orders to report for active duty as a second lieutenant just a week before my call-up in the draft to report as a buck private. A close call, that one.

Six months later, I had my overseas orders. I flew to Tokyo for processing to Korea. The paperwork at Camp Drake in Tokyo took about three weeks, so once again, to my delight, I spent most of that time touring Tokyo and Yokohama, this time with fellow junior officers. I could not believe the transformation. Evidence of bomb damage had largely vanished. It was clear that Japan was rapidly recovering from the war. I was impressed . . . but also deeply intrigued. How could Japan recover so quickly after such a terrible beating? As I read more about Japan's history, other questions arose. How had Japan managed their great leap forward from a backward and largely isolated, feudal agricultural nation in 1868 to a world industrial power by 1905—a mere 38 years? Japan's rise to the status of world power came about, of course, because in a little over a year, Japan defeated the Russian army and sank nearly the whole Russian fleet. That, and World War II had proved to me the Japanese knew how to fight. But to me as an economics major, the big question was: What force drove Japan to make such drastic changes in their economy *and* enabled them to do all that so quickly?

That question became the topic of my doctoral dissertation when I returned to graduate school after getting out of the army. What brought the question back to mind after leaving the Far East was a book by Max Weber entitled *The Protestant Ethic and the Spirit of Capitalism*. Weber claimed the Calvinist work ethic, often called the Puritan work ethic, had spiritually energized the many Calvinist entrepreneurs who brought about the industrial revolution and who invented bottom-up free enterprise capitalism in the process.

Talcott Parsons had only just translated Weber into English and it was an academic hit. The people studying management at the University of Washington's Graduate School of Business, where I was enrolled, seemed as impressed as I was. But mainstream economists such as Paul Samuelson of MIT dismissed Weber. Still, having seen for myself Japan's cultural drive in action, I wondered if some spiritual or emotional explanation also lay behind Japan's dynamic success. I concluded there was. So I wanted to entitle my dissertation, *The Samurai Ethic and the Spirit of Japitalism*. Of course my dissertation committee vetoed that one. They did agree to the much more prosaic title, *Cultural Values and Economic Growth: A Case Study of Japan*. (Case studies had become all the rage in business schools during that era.)

It was my research on Japan that first led me into a maverick mindset. The Japanese rejected the West's construct of "economic man"—a nonsocial, selfish individualist and also a creature of pure reason who always has complete information available upon which to make purely rational but selfish decisions. To them, the Western belief in such a mythical creature was a prime example of "occidental inscrutability." Instead, the Japanese put great value, not just on hard work, but also on loyalty and family feeling. The first book I read when researching my topic was James C. Abegglen's little book, *The Japanese Factory: Aspects of Its Social System*. He claimed the closest American thing to the spirit of a Japanese factory was a college fraternity. That thought blew me away.

Economists, I soon discovered, dismissed all this as a legacy of Japanese feudalism. Perhaps so, but that did not mean that Japan's feudal approach did not work. As my research continued, I discovered that the entire September 1936 issue of *Fortune* magazine was entitled The Rising Sun in the Pacific. In almost awestruck tones *Fortune* explained how Japan's oligopolistic *zaibatsu* had slashed prices to maintain output and exports during the years 1929–1933. In so doing they leaped right over our Smoot-Hawley tariff of 1930. Thus Japan avoided unemployment during the Great Depression. Japan's employment, 1929–1933, actually rose slightly, while ours collapsed, falling 40 percent in the industrial sector. Total U.S. unemployment was only 24 percent, by virtue of the fact that farm output and employment rose slightly as farm prices fell 50 percent or more— roughly the same decrease Japan's industrial prices experienced as administered by Japan's oligopolistic industry. (Here let it be noted that Japan's financial sector collapsed in1990 from the same kind of dumbness found in America. But that collapse did not spread to industrial firms.)

Now my Keynesian economics professors had earlier convinced me that Keynes had proved the failure of Say's Law of Markets. Say's Law held that supply creates its demand and thus involuntary unemployment was not possible under *laissez-faire*. What more evidence did one need than the Great Depression to show that a self-regulated market could not produce stable full employment as Say's Law promised? My Keynesian professors also informed us that Gardiner S. Means had shown that agricultural prices had conformed to Say's Law only because farmers are so small and so many in number that they must live in a purely competitive market, forced to accept an auction price or else get nothing. Oligopolies, according to Means, have so much market power they can set (administer) their own prices and they do so to protect profit margins. But, I asked my professor, what about Japan? How could the *zaibatsu* slash prices and protect profits too? "A different culture," he responded, feudal and all that. Japan's system doesn't apply here, he said, so forget it. I did not forget it, but I knew enough not to challenge *Herr Doktor* Professor. He regarded Keynes as some kind of god and I depended on the good professor for a good grade.

I did not reject all of what Keynes said. Still, in light of both our farm sector and Japan's oligopolistic industrial sector, I concluded that Say's Law had not failed. If costs were flexible his law worked as advertised. Indeed both these quite different sectors had the same thing going for them. Both sectors had the inherently flexible labor costs of partnership. Say's Law, after all, promised full employment only if labor's unit costs were flexible enough to allow for price cuts in a slump, and both American farmers and Japanese workers satisfied Say's criteria and thus conformed to his law.

I spent the next 20-odd years often wondering why neither liberals nor conservatives ever got interested in a partnership between capital and labor. It is a free enterprise alternative to the toxic adversarial relationship that only economists seem to defend. (Operating managers grumble about it all the time.) My research on this book allowed me at long last to see why most people in the finance sector did not object. I was stunned to discover that Wall Street actually has a deeply vested interest in defending the myth of the economic man. They love that adversarial relationship. That relationship and the mythical and nonsensical economic man both help Wall Street justify the huge bonuses they and their corrupt clients, both liberal and conservative, suck out of the economy under cover of *laissez-faire*. Not only that, it gives their greed a philosophical cover that "greed is good." I concluded that the folks on Wall Street realized they could never get away with such gross greed at the top level in a real-world partnership. They needed a mechanistic, philosophical cover and the commodity theory of labor to justify their work: unfriendly takeovers, leveraged buyouts, selling off parts or closing them down and selling off the physical assets, shipping the jobs of hirelings abroad. It is easier to break out the champagne and exchange high fives when firing thousands of people if they can be dehumanized into faceless hirelings or so many undifferentiated and expendable units of labor now become "dead wood."

That behavior could self-righteously be justified under the favorite cover of increasing shareholder value. People as hirelings just do not count in that equation, but people as partners would count very much. Working partners who had a voice in the partnership agreement would never put up with huge bonuses for senior partners entirely at the expense of the working partners. They would never stand for the obscene greed Wall Street was promoting for itself and those at the top and particularly for those in finance. They would not allow contracts that let guys like Stan O'Neal of Merrill Lynch walk away from the firm he nearly destroyed with a payoff of $150 million.

That is why, I concluded, Wall Street worked so hard to neutralize the real reforms American management had been trying to implement during the 1980s and 1990s in response to Japanese competition. The quality reforms were implemented under Dr. W. Edwards Deming. Deming was an American consultant to Japanese industry who came under our military occupation to help Japan recover. He later brought those reforms over here to revitalize our operating economy over the 20 years from 1980 to 2000. But the repeal of Glass-Steagall in 1999 largely stopped those reforms cold. In fact, many reforms were often reversed in an orgy of top-level greed run wild. That greed was as always justified under the high-sounding cover of adding shareholder value. Under that cover, good companies were pulled apart and thousands of employees fired. Other times, the hired employees were sacrificed on the altar of globalization as their jobs were shipped to Mexico, China, South Korea, Malaysia, or India. Working partners might do some of that, but not on the scale of the last decade.

Still, one other thing needs to be said. While the trade unions often threw fits about management greed, and especially about jobs going abroad, unions never came close to advocating that their members become working partners with capital. The reason is clear enough. Such a partnership would effectively dissolve the very cause that justifies the unions' existence. Why would partners need a union if they were happy with the partnership agreement? The adversarial relationship, in short, does for trade unions what the commodity theory of labor does for Wall Street. Ironically, these competing interest groups have thus far succeeded in blocking efforts at real reform that could benefit both.

So what is to be done to put things right? Let me give my short answer up front. First, bring back some form of Glass-Steagall to eliminate most of the greed, and reregulate the financial sector to constrain leveraged speculation. Do that and we will get no more bubbles that sooner or later must burst. Nor will we get the greed and the moral corruption that goes with them.

Second, encourage the conversion of corporations to limited liability partnerships between stockholders and employees. Given the inherently flexible unit labor costs of partnerships, our corporations could compete with foreign rivals in ways they cannot now. Partnerships also provide employment stability that reduces the need for government welfare. There would be no bout of mass unemployment as there was in the thirties. To encourage the formation of such partnerships, eliminate the corporate profits tax on corporations that convert to partnerships that conform to the legal definition of one. After all, partnerships have never been subject to a corporate profits tax. (The partners pay the personal income tax rate on partnership income.) Meanwhile, continue to levy the corporate profits tax on those firms that remain cost-rigid bureaucracies staffed mainly with cost-rigid hirelings. (I discuss other desirable reforms in the five Appendices at the end of the book.)

Let me end the story of my journey as a conservative maverick on this note. When things are going well, I now see, there is no realistic hope that such changes as I just outlined will take place. If we are making money, who needs them? But now that 2008 has again proved that leveraged speculation encourages untrammeled greed and investment bubbles destined to burst, I feel some optimism. Most drunks must crash or hit bottom before they convert to sobriety; thanks to both liberal and conservative policies, we Americans have come to the end of a 30-year credit bender, crashing into a huge wall of debt. Perhaps now we will find the political will to save our free enterprise system and its relative freedoms.

Otherwise, I fear that we will fall into a fascist-like NRA solution that the New Deal launched in 1933 before the Supreme Court declared it unconstitutional. (The NRA threw a dry cleaner into jail for three months because he charged 35 cents instead of the NRA's prescribed 40 cents to dry-clean a suit.)[2] If not fascism, then we might well slip into a creeping socialism. Fascist and socialist economies both take a top down approach. Fascism and socialism came to Europe by popular demand to restore economic stability and we came close to doing that in the New Deal. The stability comes, of course, at considerable cost to personal freedom including the freedom to innovate and start new firms. Those freedoms must be preserved to maintain a viable free enterprise system, but such freedoms must conform to the rules of the game or chaos will follow. Dictatorship usually follows such chaos, and by popular demand.

NOTES

1. Wallace, William McDonald. *Techno-Cultural Evolution: Cycles of Creation and Conflict*. Dulles, VA: Potomac Books, 2006.

2. Goldberg, Jonah. *Liberal Fascism*. New York: Broadway Books, 2009, p. 155. Goldberg also gives a fascinating account of America's near fascist episode under President Woodrow Wilson, during and shortly after World War I.

INTRODUCTION

Leveraged speculation brought down the whole global financial structure in 2008. It is *the* strategy for getting rich quick by using other people's money to leverage your own money by a factor of as much as 10, and recently by a factor of 100. That prospect clearly ignites excitement, or in the words of Alan Greenspan, "irrational exuberance." As it happens, when you leverage your own money, you also leverage your own greed to get rich quick. Leveraged greed often causes us to suspend common sense. Seeing a chance for getting rich quick often amplifies our greed by addictive injections of our own adrenalin. Lustfully hyped up, we resist seeing the truth. We want no rain on this fantasy parade of great wealth and we are thus prone to dismiss storm warnings of danger.

Leveraged speculation drives up asset prices artificially by pushing prices well beyond the asset's underlying value. Let us be crystal clear. Such price rises are not the normal workings of a rational market. If the price rises far beyond the rational point of underlying value then a price bubble is created that *has* to burst sooner or later. When it bursts, the illusion of rising wealth vanishes at once, but the very real build up of the debt that drove up those prices so far beyond reason remains. That remaining debt, minus the now vanished artificial value of the assets, caused the 2008 collapse of the global financial structure.

All that had happened before, in 1929. After that crash, few doubted the dangers of leveraged speculation. Moreover, the whole idea of *laissez-faire* then lost its appeal because of all the ruined lives and suicides. It could no longer serve as the supreme ideal of free-enterprise capitalism. For the next 40-odd years *laissez-faire* was viewed not as serious theory, but rather an antique conception dating back to the eighteenth century of Adam Smith, before most of the complexities of the industrial revolution had surfaced. Congress for its part had put severe constraints on leverage and the banking system in general. Today, some conservatives argue that those constraints slowed our recovery from the Great Depression. There may be some truth to that charge, because the economy did not recover to its 1929 level until we entered World War II. But, having entered that war, the newly stabilized financial system immediately proved its worth. The nation had absolutely no trouble financing the war, unlike the difficulties it encountered with the far lesser challenge of World War I. At the end of the war, many economists and business leaders expected a resumption of depression. But instead of depression, the nation began to experience a boom that lasted until the early seventies with only a few mild recessions. By 1958 Professor John Kenneth Galbraith had published his best-selling book, *The Affluent Society*. During all that time *laissez-faire* was under a cloud and the banking system was tightly regulated.

By about 1980, however, *laissez-faire* came roaring back as serious theory. After all, Keynesianism, the god that replaced *laissez-faire*, had itself begun to fail. Stagflation (rising rates of both inflation and unemployment) had surfaced, a condition supposedly impossible under Keynesianism, since, according to standard definitions inflation is caused by too much demand and unemployment is caused by too little. So how could we have both at the same time? Many liberals, moreover, were also getting sick of too much regulation and Jimmy Carter's presidency had seemed to fail. The entrepreneurial spirit seemed dead and the high tax rates Keynesian theory had justified seemed to squelch that spirit of enterprise. Many of us conservatives began to feel that we had been far too hard on *laissez-faire*. It deserved another chance.

So, Adam Smith neckties suddenly appeared (I still have mine). The cry for tax cuts went out under Reagan, for whom I voted. Ronald Reagan inspired a renewed energy among conservatives, and that included me. But as far as financial regulation was concerned, something else happened, largely out of public view. In 1973, two young PhDs, Fischer Black and Myron Scholes, published a technical paper featuring a highly complex mathematical formula that described how to price stock options (a form of financial derivative) using leverage.[1] They claimed that the use of their formula would reduce or even eliminate the risk of leveraged speculation (buying options is speculating on what will happen to the stock price from which the option is derived).

Before that paper came out, speculating in options had been a minor part of the game in financial markets. After that paper came out, action in the market for options and other derivatives skyrocketed. Now, suddenly, the game had supposedly changed. Mainframe computers had allowed Black and Scholes to formulate sophisticated mathematical strategies to manage and reduce the implicit risk of leverage. And if leverage was no longer terribly risky, why not deregulate the financial sector? Why not allow much greater freedom to innovate many new ways to speculate? If you can avoid the risk, then leveraged speculation can indeed increase wealth. Everyone benefits. So, in a rush of broadly based enthusiasm, America began the process of financial deregulation that brought back a version of *laissez-faire*.

That deregulation was the very disruption that created a chaotic new order in finance that included release from the constraints on leveraged speculation. A competitive rush to exploit these opportunities soon began. (Ecologists refer to this as "ecological release.")

Speculative bubbles appeared almost at once, beginning with the savings and loan banks. In 1987, as that bubble was bursting, the stock market collapsed. A year later, Myron Scholes, who had now won a Nobel Prize, saw his own Long Term Capital Management Hedge Fund collapse following the default of Russia. Meanwhile, the dot-com boom was in full force, only to go bust in 2000–2001. Despite this dismal record demonstrating that the dangers of leverage had not been mathematically contained, the leverage band kept on playing, louder than ever. The top command of the financial sector continued to insist they could manage the risk implicit in leveraged speculation. We were assured that these geniuses backed by brilliant academic nerds and geeks could use leverage to create ever expanding wealth even as savings all but vanished into debt. Thus the call for reregulation was dismissed. Had it ended there, we still might have avoided the super collapse in 2008. (By 1990, after the explosion of junk-mail credit cards that featured revolving credit, I had become skeptical about freewheeling finance.)

But another "disruption" to the ecology of finance took place in the mid-nineties that spelled doom in 2008. In the interests of social engineering and "social justice," this disruption was suspending financial common sense in the setting of standards, terms, and interest rates for mortgage loans. For example, traditional guidelines held that a borrower should put 20 percent down, pay closing costs with cash, pay about 6 percent interest, and limit the mortgage to about two and half times annual income. In the interest of social engineering, these standards were cast aside to make it possible for the poor and disadvantaged to buy homes in what came to be called the "subprime market." Borrowers in many cases did not need to prove they even had an income; these were the so-called NINJA loans for No Income, No Job, or Assets. Some borrowers got approved for loans with nothing down and the closing costs rolled up into the mortgage itself. Many loans had very low interest rates for the first few years before being adjusted upward. In some cases only interest had to be paid for the first five years before payments began on the principle itself. NINJA lending (as shorthand for the whole array of such approaches) was mainly a creature of liberal thinking. We will explore it later in the book, but we see here a sort of Faustian bargain between liberals and conservatives. Liberals in Congress implicitly agreed—despite deep reservations—to accept financial deregulation and the unbridled use of leveraged speculation if conservatives—despite deep reservations—agreed to go along with NINJA lending in the interests of social justice. What came about were the very worst features of both ideologies, a perfect storm.

Thus began the killer housing bubble that burst in 2008. When it burst, it brought down the entire global financial structure. Depending on the course of future events, 2008 may come to be seen as capitalism's extinction event. Even if capitalism—or at least free enterprise—survives in some form, 2008 will almost certainly put a black cloud over *laissez-faire*.

Just before writing this introduction, my wife and I listened to a talk in Indian Wells, California, by a Nobel Prize winning economist, Professor Paul Krugman. He gave a good partial overview of the events and decisions leading up to 2008. But he ignored much of importance. Professor Krugman did not mention the Black and Scholes equation or even refer indirectly to it. Krugman clearly came across as a quant kind of guy and said John Maynard Keynes was his hero. Krugman did not even mention the word leverage. Of course he referred to the bubbles that burst, but did not go beyond Alan Greenspan's famous euphemism, "irrational exuberance" to explain them. But it helps to know why such exuberance comes about in the first place. What is the psychology behind it? To answer that question let us consider why *all* speculation based on high leverage tends to generate "irrational exuberance" and the amplification of greed.

Let us begin by assuming a normal (rational) housing market with normal terms of credit (how much down, how long to pay), credit standards (who can qualify for the loan), and mortgage interest rates. Now we disrupt that normal market by easing credit terms (nothing down, etc.), abolishing credit standards (if you say you have a job, we believe you and will not check), and offering very low initial interest rates. In short, we set up conditions for letting leveraged speculation run loose and that makes it much easier than before for poor people to enter the market to buy a home. These new customers (some solid, to be sure, but as a matter of statistical certainty, many of them deadbeats) can now buy homes. As they come rushing into the market to do so, their new demand pushes up the price of existing housing. Current homeowners are soon delighted to see they now have much more equity. They can (and many did) use that equity to get a home equity loan to buy that new car, take that vacation, send the kids to college, or do an extensive remodel. This immediately converted equity into more debt. Meanwhile, the low rates and soft terms quickly began to attract investors and speculators as well as prospective homeowners. Stocks had dipped, so money moved out of the stock market into housing. Stories began to circulate about the killings some people were making in the housing market. "Gee, I bought a $300,000 house with nothing down on a low adjustable rate loan, and in six months the market had pushed the price up by 15 percent!! I could afford that on unemployment compensation!!"

Those stories brought in still more investors, bidding up prices even further. And so on. One guideline to the underlying value of a house or condo is how much rent it can fetch. (When pressure pushes rents higher, it makes sense that house prices will rise as well.) The traditional guideline is that the capital value of a house is about 100 times what it will fetch as a monthly rental. By 2005, this ratio had gotten way beyond reason. Some houses that would bring in only about $2,500 as a rental were selling for $1,000,000, suggesting the price of the house was four times too high.

By 2005, housing prices were so high that people earning a middle-class income could no longer afford a modest house. And since property taxes increased as the assessed values of houses rose, more and more older homeowners found themselves hard pressed to pay the higher rates. Smart investors who saw all this began to sell off. They paid off their broker or other loans, took their net profits, and ran. Once that happened, the game was up. Again, the logic of leverage—that is, betting with other people's money—requires ever ascending asset prices to sustain the bubble once prices rise above the underlying fundamental value. Greed encourages many to believe this will happen indefinitely. (This is a whole different kind of market they assure themselves.) But when prices stop rising, fear almost immediately replaces greed. Stark terror soon sets in among investors who have borrowed heavily. Instantly, they are in trouble; the first to see that truth begin to sell off to limit their losses. Panic begins. The bubble has now burst and the investors who thought they had gotten rich quick are suddenly broke and often deeply in debt to boot. They are left with a now huge debt and no assets to support it. Many are ruined along with the many highly leveraged banks, business firms, hedge funds and other investment funds, insurance companies, and stock brokers. They all crash. Here we see the truth of Greenspan's complaint that once a bubble began to form, the Federal Reserve Board (the Fed) could not stop it without collapsing it. The trick of course is not stopping it, but preventing it.

And all that is more or less what happened in 2008, culminating in October. Huge debt remained, minus trillions of dollars of vanished asset value needed to sustain the debt. All that happened thanks to the subprime market brought about by that Faustian bargain. It left the global financial structure in ruins, loaded with debt sustained by now vanished assets.

Here, let us note the difference between a boom that goes bust and a bubble that bursts. It is important to understand that boom and bust is an integral part of natural evolution. But bubbles that burst are not: they are man-made events driven by greed that is nourished by false theory or assumptions and that set historical precedent aside by noting, "This time it's different." The setting may, of course, always be different. But the behavior remains constant.

The main difference between bubble and bust, however, is that after the bust a great deal of asset value remains. Boom and bust became descriptions of economic evolution only after sufficient innovations had come into being to bring forth the industrial revolution and capitalism, both based on new technology. A good example comes from the railroads, the nation's first "big business." As technology continued to advance, the railroads continued to grow and expand for about 50 years beginning from about 1830. Much of the financing came from Europeans who purchased stocks and bonds in the railroads. But by 1890 the railroads now spanned the United States from coast to coast and border to border. Indeed, they had rather seriously overbuilt the network. Many railroads went bankrupt after this overexploitation and were absorbed by the larger or stronger roads. Many Europeans and other investors lost money, sometimes a great deal of money. Still, the rail network and most of the rolling stock remained in place and provided the infrastructural base upon which yet more new industries could grow.

The stronger roads at once began to curtail the dog-eat-dog, all-out *laissez-faire* competition that had left them nearly exhausted. They immediately began to form cartels and other price-fixing agreements as well as local monopolies where they could charge all that the traffic would bear. But very quickly, they were confronted by an outraged public used to paying competitive prices. Congress was soon pressured into passing the Sherman Antitrust Act, outlawing trusts and cartels along with price-fixing agreements. They also created the Interstate Commerce Commission to regulate fares and freight rates. In that way, Congress saved capitalism and allowed innovation to continue, but it did so by sharply curtailing *laissez-faire* for the common carriers. We will expand on this history in later chapters.

With this overview, let us now describe the rest of the book. In Part One, we will explore the collapse of 2008 in more detail. Chapter 1 will begin with how Black and Scholes claimed to have found a mathematical formula that would allow investors to avoid the risks implicit in leveraged speculation. In Chapter 2 we see how that hope played a big part in the financial deregulation of the late seventies and early eighties. Chapter 3 shows how deregulation engendered a new embrace of *laissez-faire*, which later led to the amplification of greed and a suspension of common sense and historical wisdom. Chapter 4 takes us through the preliminary series of bubbles and bursts after deregulation, including the savings and loan banks. We will also look at the explosion of revolving credit cards, and the dot-com boom and bust. Outside the United States we will see the big Japanese stock and real estate bubble of 1980 that went bust in 1990. In Chapter 5 we set the stage for the Faustian bargain. We will see why Congress decided to empower the Association of Community Organizations for Reform Now (ACORN) to pressure banks to soften credit terms to avoid accusations that traditional terms were simply a racist mechanism to deny blacks and other deserving minorities access to home ownership. In Chapter 6 we come to the Faustian bargain itself. We will see how an ill-considered liberal social engineering program and an equally ill-considered conservative embrace of leveraged speculation conspired to form, and ultimately explode, the subprime mortgage bubble. In Chapter 7 we drill down into the detail of the bubble's formation and its later bursting wide open. Included are the roles played by Congress, Fannie Mae, Freddie Mac, the hedge funds, and the Federal Reserve Board. We will see a pervasive tolerance by both conservatives and liberals for rampant greed in the financial sector. This chapter completes the story of the October 2008 collapse.

In Part Two we return to Darwin's Gap. Chapter 8 looks more closely at Charles Lyell's geological theory of uniformitarianism that Charles Darwin embraced thus to obscure how evolution actually works and help set the stage for bubbles that burst. In Chapter 9 we see how Steven J. Gould and Niles Eldredge developed the evidence to disprove uniformitarianism in evolution allowing us to identify the FROCA process that governs both cultural and biological evolution. Chapter 10 looks at why different behavior patterns emerge in the punctuation phase compared to the equilibrium phase of evolution. We will see why we often set aside the rules in punctuation of frontiers of survival, while we demand close observance of the rules in equilibrium. We will see that most of the social sciences do not yet see how such behavioral differences arise from evolution. We will also see why economists and business managers need to be very clear about these differences, but also why they often do not want to. In Part Three, we look at the future possibilities. In Chapter 11 we look at what we need to do to Get It Right. We will see how we need to reregulate the financial sector along the lines of 1935–1980. We will see how we need to switch from a labor force made up mostly of cost-rigid hirelings, to cost-flexible partners. We will see how we need to apply antitrust laws in a way to limit the size of firms so that they do not become "too big to fail." If we take these steps, we can get beyond untrammeled *laissez-faire* and its bursting bubbles. We will also see how, at the same time, we can avoid the usual alternative of a highly authoritarian government such as fascism or socialism.

We then take a look at several issues that did not directly contribute to the collapse of 2008, but nevertheless require solutions if we are to achieve a free-enterprise system that avoids the extremes. Appendix A shows us *that real health care costs less, not more.* It explains why both liberals and conservatives deliberately obscured this fact with a semantic trick by calling medical insurance "health care." Next, Appendix B looks at post-2008 globalization, at the threats it poses as well as how to deal with them. Appendix C examines the need for immigration reform to resolve the problem of illegal immigrants. Appendix D considers how to deal with environmental protection without trashing the economy. Appendix E looks at the connection between energy independence and Islamic terrorism, and how political correctness strives to obscure the truth.

The bottom line, however, is that unless we make the reforms outlined in Chapter 11, we will not likely cope effectively with health care, globalization, immigration, energy, or the environment. And failing to solve those problems, we will likely become a nation in steep decline, beset with internal political gridlock, an inability to compete with China and other countries, and growing internal corruption and discontent. But it is not too late to reverse the "decline and fall of the American economy." We can put it right, but first we have to learn from our mistakes. We have to look at the real world and what has actually happened. We must take off the ideological blinders that have led both conservatives and liberals to create often disastrous policies.

NOTE

1. For a good description of the Black and Scholes Model, see Ferguson, Niall. *The Ascent of Money: A Financial History of the World.* New York: The New Penguin Press, 2008, pp. 320–328.

Part I

THE 2008 COLLAPSE AND ITS ORIGINS

Chapter 1

BLACK AND SCHOLES'S RISK MANAGEMENT FORMULA

D r. Myron Scholes defined the Black and Scholes theory in a *New York Times* interview with Deborah Solomon on May 14, 2009: "It is an equation that prices options on common stocks and provides a methodology to value options on securities generally. It can be used to measure risk and transfer risk."

When she followed with another question—"In retrospect, is it fair to say that the idea that banks could manage risk was a total illusion?"—Scholes responded: "What you are saying is negative. Life is positive too. Every side of a coin has another side." I interpret Dr. Scholes' evasive response to Ms. Solomon's very clear question as a yes: it was a total illusion. The crash of 2008 was resounding proof.

But it was an illusion born in the context of the times. So, before we go further with Black and Scholes, it is first necessary to set the stage for their work, to flesh out the cultural context of the times. They did not construct this stage, or create the culture. Rather, in the classic way of evolution, they merely adapted to it. The construction of that stage and the onset of a new culture celebrating debt began under the influence of Britain's John Maynard Keynes, later to become Lord Keynes, to many, the most famous economist of the twentieth century. Keynes helped create a new economic context by inducing a paradigm shift from eighteenth-century classical to twentieth-century neo-classical economics. In so doing, Keynes single-handedly created a new discipline called "macroeconomics."

John Maynard Keynes made mathematical analysis of economic events academically popular. His 1936 book, *The General Theory of Employment, Interest, and Money* was an abstract analysis of the Great Depression. That book was destined to be Keynes's masterwork. It made Keynes the twentieth century's most influential economist by far, according to many economists, among them Nobel Prize winner Paul Krugman, who holds Keynes as his idol.

Briefly, Keynes argued that Say's Law of Markets fails to apply in a slump. Say's Law states that given flexible costs and prices, free markets assure full employment of all resources. In effect, if prices are not fixed, supply will create its own demand. More on Keynes's critique later. Here we should note that Keynes made his case not on the basis of actual data of the Great Depression, but by mathematical logic applied to his assumptions. Like Ricardo and Marx before him, he let abstract logic trump actual data. (Keynes's theory falls apart when applied to the actual data of that time. That data actually confirms rather than refutes Say's Law. I developed this analysis in my 1995 journal article "The Great Depression Reconsidered and Its Implications for Today.")[1] We will look at this in more depth later.

His *General Theory* was difficult to read and follow because, as we see later when we look at Black and Scholes's famous equation, most of us bog down if confronted by thickets of algebra not of our own making. That is why it was not until about 1948 (after Keynes had died at a fairly early age) that Keynesian theory began to motivate economists to adopt his "macroeconomic" approach. (Macroeconomics did not exist until Keynes created it.) It was not just the passage of time, however, that led to this conversion. A good part of this shift occurred because of the wartime invention of the mainframe computer. As early mainframes improved and their software became more sophisticated, wannabe math majors by the hundreds began to shift to an economics major. ("Pure mathematicians" in those days looked down on powerful computers claiming that using electronic computers to crunch numbers by brute force would seduce mathematicians to grow lazy in thinking about the underlying mathematical logic.) (They actually had a point. Shortly before I retired from Boeing, the USSR imploded and the Cold War ended. For the first time, Boeing engineers could freely travel to Russia. Many were eager to go because Boeing engineers had learned that Russian mathematicians, lacking the easy access to computers of Americans, had made some major breakthroughs in basic math concepts important to engineers.)

From about 1948, when Paul Samuelson first published his landmark text, *Economics*, people who liked math began shifting to economics without feeling guilty about using computers. It was just too tedious to create any complex mathematical or statistical model for economic forecasting. Even a simple least-squares trend analysis can be tedious and time consuming if done by hand. (With a computer and the right software, you can enter the data, then hit the button, and before you can blink, you have the R2 and trend line.)

The big rush came after 1960, when Robert McNamara, after rising quickly up the ladder at Ford Motor Co. using quantitative methods, and just becoming president of the company accepted newly elected President John F. Kennedy's invitation to become Secretary of Defense. McNamara introduced his quantitative methods at the Pentagon, where, already, during World War II, he had served the Air Force as a quantitative "whiz kid." He insisted on expressing everything in numbers and using computer models to solve all problems. Many of his reforms were certainly needed; some were long overdue; and in the end, Pentagon operations were markedly transformed. But McNamara disdained any wisdom that could not be expressed numerically. He was clear about all that. McNamara was a self-confessed neo-positivist, a school of philosophy claiming that if you cannot express your position numerically it has no useful meaning.

McNamara was also clear that the mainframe computer made this level of quantification practical for the first time in history. He was convinced that the awesome computing power of the mainframe had finally made it possible to make detailed and accurate forecasts. Given the power to forecast accurately, it becomes logical and necessary to plan according to that forecast. In business, such plans include the scheduling of production, and that schedule calls for allocating money, men, and material according to that plan. Only top management can perform this job McNamara insisted. Having made the forecast and planned accordingly, management must issue the commands to implement production and then monitor for compliance by the use of controls to assure that the plans are followed. Forecasting, planning, command, and control became the name of McNamara's computer-era game. Given all that, McNamara also felt that the burgeoning human relations school then prevalent in many university business schools and in some business firms, was just so much touchy-feely fluff.

That "fluff" came into being when researchers discovered in the now famous Hawthorne Studies at Western Electric that workers had far more influence over productive efficiency than the adherents of Frederick Winslow Taylor's school of scientific management had suspected.[2]

For example, workers were routinely able to frustrate the "time and motion" studies designed to improve their productivity. Moreover, workers were easily able to bring pressure to bear on their peers either to enhance or retard productivity. The human relations school as such emerged when Harvard Business School professors took this and similar findings to heart and urged worker participation in decision making. They insisted that workers deserved far more respect than the time and motion studies ever considered necessary. People, in this new human relations view, were to be seen as a business firm's most important resource and treated as such.

McNamara did not put down human relations as crudely as I have suggested, but he thought the mainframe had made such thinking outdated and largely irrelevant. After all, if the top command has all the information needed to make the plans, what use is input from the lower levels who themselves have no access to such information except through top management? Elsewhere I have paraphrased his argument as follows:

I know that people do not like to be told what to do or that their input is irrelevant. But now that we have the means to make accurate forecasts, this new power allows management to make plans that can avoid such catastrophes as the Great Depression, when millions were thrown out of work. By following those plans, everyone will have far better job security. Consider, for example, if a ship must leave port at high tide to pass the bar and get out to sea, and we already know when high tide comes, what good does it do to debate the time of departure?

Once again, only top management and their professional staff can make these forecasts and see the Big Picture.[3]

By the mid-sixties McNamara's thinking had largely swept the field in both corporate and academic America. I witnessed the beginning of this shift while in graduate school at the University of Washington. When I enrolled in 1956, the human relations school was all the rage. It remained so in 1957 as well. But in 1958 human relations was suddenly put on the defensive when other departments began getting access to new mainframes. "You can't use human relations to schedule production," the operations folks insisted. "You can't use it to make financial plans," the finance folks chimed in. Fierce debates among the faculty erupted—which I tried to dodge because professors on both sides of this issue could have torpedoed my doctorate.

By the time I went to Boeing in 1960 the quantitative approach had seized the high academic ground. Once mainframes had become widely available, the quant folks began to run research circles around the suddenly outdated human relations school, which was all case study method and taught few principles. Cynics from trade unions put it down as "more milk from contented cows." Finance cynics said the whole thing could be summed in three words, "Don't fire Mary." I had been converted to the human relations view, so I had to lay low.

McNamara's success turning Ford around in the fifties (after the awful mess left by old Henry in his dotage) was widely cited as proof of the power of the quantitative methods. The Depression aside, economic history soon became a backwater among academic economists after Keynes, and much the same thing happened to the human relations faculties in Business Schools after the mainframe computer revolution.

McNamara's defense of top down command and control in part mimicked the defense Frederic Taylor and his followers had long made for scientific management. "We are not your enemies; we are trying to improve your job security and that can come only from improving your productivity." But now instead of calling it "scientific management" the quantifiers called it "management science." Either way, it was billed as something management is doing to you for "your own good." Assuming that computers did enable economists to make accurate economic forecasts, McNamara's insistence on top down command and control through management science was plausible. The assumption proved false, of course, but McNamara's conclusions followed logically from the premise.

Today as a matter of science, we know that a linear and mechanistic world exists only as a fantasy of logic, dependent on various false assumptions to make the logic work. Still it is a fantasy. And in fact, a new scientific paradigm that destroyed rigorous linear positivism had already emerged 33 years earlier—quantum physics. Ironically, quantum physics is the very science that made electronic computers possible, those marvelous machines that led McNamara to put such great faith in positivism. Still, it now seems naive to have ever fantasized such a mechanistic world. It was to be a world of rational objectivity where linear programming, queuing theory, critical path scheduling, and decision trees would give us accurate answers all the time. In this highly rational world, subjectivity and intuition are banished. In strong mechanistic determinism, there is no room for free will. Indeed, as an undergrad, I half convinced myself, based on Pierre Laplace's thought experiment (see below), that we human beings were simply mechanistic automatons whose lives had been predetermined but who lived under a delusion of free will because, in accord with Darwin's process of natural selection, that delusion improved our chances of survival. Even today, some Darwinists continue to make that argument.

But of course determinism had always had its critics. One of them poked fun at it with a limerick.

> There once was a man who said damn!!
> It seems I most certainly am
> a creature that moves in determinant groves;
> I'm not even a bus,
> I'm a tram.

Such determinism owes much to Pierre Laplace, a noted mathematician and early positivist of the French Enlightenment. He claimed that if we had a computer big enough to track the velocity and position of all the material particles of the universe, we could use Newton's three laws of motion, inverse square law of gravity, and his method of calculus to forecast everything that will ever happen because present conditions will determine future conditions. We could also, working backward, lay down the complete chain of causality of everything that ever had happened to bring the world to the present moment. In this view, my writing this book and your reading it was predetermined by the initial arrangement of matter at the time of the Big Bang. Laplace of course did not imagine that such a computer would ever exist; he was merely conducting a thought experiment. McNamara, however, seems to have looked upon early mainframe computers such as the IBM 360 as the marvel that had brought Mr. Laplace's linear and mechanistic world into being.

A central tenet of quantum physics is Heisenberg's uncertainty principle. It states that to determine the velocity of a particle, one must disturb its position, and to fix its position one must disturb its velocity. In short to observe something at the subatomic level changes its future in one way or another. Heisenberg put forth that principle in 1927, decades before McNamara went to Ford or became Secretary of Defense. We might concede Heisenberg's principle as a truth for subatomic particles, but surely Newton's laws must continue to rule in the macro world in which we live. That, at least, had been my view. In the early seventies, however, a new theory was emerging, a nonlinear theory of chaos in our macro world.

Chaos theory explores the real nonlinear world neither Laplace or McNamara ever acknowledged. In the classical Newtonian world of modern science, math was seen as almost entirely linear. But it gradually became apparent that a nonlinear world also existed, a world entirely foreign to Lyell and Darwin's uniformitarianism, or to Laplace and McNamara's world of positivism. In this chaotic world of turbulence, nonlinear chaos is the routine stuff of life. Here, the tiniest change in initial conditions can, via positive feedback loops, keep on amplifying to bring about huge changes in later outcomes. Meteorologists at MIT coined the whimsical term "butterfly effect" to describe it.[4] (If a butterfly flaps its wings in the Amazon under the right circumstances, a positive feedback loop can continue to amplify the slightly disturbed air current until it has become a tornado in Kansas six months later.) The implication is that, to forecast the weather accurately six months out, you need to track every butterfly on earth, which would so load the earth up with sensing instruments, they themselves would change the weather.

But before chaos theory came to light, the linear quantitative rage swept through business and academia, powered by an explosive development of mainframe technology and software beginning about 1960. Almost at once, economists, corporate staff planners, linear systems analysts, and similarly skilled professionals were recruited in great numbers into the large corporations, promising they could make accurate linear predictions. Needless to say, chaos theory was not greeted very warmly by these cadres when it first came out. They ignored it as long as they could because this new science told them the one thing they did not want to hear, namely that the future was inherently uncertain. It was a tropical deluge threatening to rain down on their deterministic quantitative parade and wash it away. Chaos theory clearly blew away Mr. McNamara's rationale for an arrogant, know-it-all policy based on a rigorously linear system of top down command and control. His whole approach depended on the certainty of predicting the future, and that certainty is something that chaos theory precludes.

But with so much at stake, the new science showing that nonlinear turbulence precludes accurate predictions of the future at first got a cold welcome at best.

I know, because I went through this crisis while still at Boeing. Unwittingly, we had all become infected with McNamara's positivism. We had tried to use some aspects of chaos, or complexity, theory at Boeing to make better forecasts—but without success. And, I must confess, up to that time I implicitly assumed a deterministic future. That is to say, if, in 1980, I had to forecast airline traffic for 2000, I accepted as given that the 2000 traffic level had already been determined, in the sense that it was subject to certain determination in 1980. My job was to come up with clever and plausible forecasting algorithms to get us from here to there. Even so, I was also aware that most of my forecasting successes had come not from the quantitative methods per se, but from insights rooted in "backwater" historical analysis.

Thus it was a shock to me when in the mid-eighties I read James Gleick's book, *Chaos Theory*. The first chapter, "The Butterfly Effect," laid me low. I felt deeply depressed that I had spent most of my professional career in what amounted to false practice. The future, I learned, is not deterministic, it is contingent. Moreover, since 1980, the economy was in turmoil because of the second oil price crisis.

We had adjusted our forecasts to show ever rising oil prices, and then the price collapsed. Economists had no sooner adjusted to rising oil prices than they had to adapt to an abrupt change to much lower oil prices. Most were left hanging out there with forecasts of oil prices well north of $40.00 per barrel when the price of oil plummeted to a low of $7.00 before settling in for a while at $16.00.

The economy, rocked by unexpected—unpredicted—shocks, had just gone through a full decade of one failed forecast after another. The first shock was OPEC I of 1973 following the Arab attack on Israel in October beginning on Yom Kippur. Oil prices shot up from about $2.50 per barrel to $14.00. That jump immediately ruined every national economic forecast in the nation. The big macro-model forecasting firms such as DRI and Wharton fell all over themselves explaining why no one could have expected them to forecast the Yom Kippur War and its political and economic aftermath.

Quite true, but it is just as true that unexpected and unforecastable events are the actual stuff of life in the real, nonlinear world of turbulence. Shock number two was OPEC II in 1978. Once again, you cannot blame forecasters for failing to foresee that the Shah of Iran would contract terminal cancer, leave the country for treatment, and thus make it possible for the Ayatollah Khomeini to return to Iran, take it over, and then take the entire diplomatic staff of the American Embassy hostage. Again every national forecast was vitiated as oil prices shot from $14 to $34 per barrel. Shock number three was Japan's sudden post-sixties ability to penetrate deeply into so many American markets such as electronic equipment and automobiles. Again, forecasts had to be quickly revised. When Lee Iacocca was asked what the solution to Japanese competition was, he offered a one-word quip—submarines.

But worse than Japan's success was the reason for it. Their success stemmed mainly from a system of labor relations that avoided the impersonal approach of using hired labor. Japan had explicitly rejected the assumption of an asocial economic man concerned only about maximizing personal profit. That was utter nonsense, the Japanese insisted. Instead Japan depended on family-like partnerships between stockholders and employees. It was clear that Japan's economic success in manufacturing depended heavily on bottom-up esprit de corps and teamwork that was natural in their family-like partnerships.

Economists, however, had consistently downplayed the significance of that approach, calling it a feudal legacy. American economists argued that this legacy was nonrational, thus temporary, and that sooner or later, Japan would be forced to embrace the West's more "rational" model of industrial relations. (While researching my doctoral dissertation on Japan's early economic history, I discovered this claim by Western economists dated from as early as 1940. For their part, the Japanese seemed more than willing to let their Western competitors mislead themselves on the labor-relations secret of Japan's industrial success.)

Business managers, however, were clearly aware of the importance of self-motivated teamwork. Many tried to create a sense of "family" in their organizations.

But economists, who had no responsibility for getting out quality production, ignored all that. Years later, when I was back in academia teaching Econ. 101, I made my students this offer: Find me a principles of economics textbook from any publisher that contains an index that mentions any of the following words: teamwork, team spirit, esprit de corps, camaraderie, or the equivalent and I will pay $10.00 cash. I have never had to pay off. (In the summer of 1980, Dr. W. Edwards Deming, an American quality consultant whom the Japanese credited with revolutionizing their product quality, presented a documentary on NBC television entitled, "If Japan can do it, why can't we?" In it Dr. Deming was scathing about the dysfunctions of American top-down command and control style of management. Deming predicted Americans could not catch up with Japanese quality unless they could match Japanese teamwork.)

Shock number four came in 1986 when oil prices nose-dived from over $30 a barrel to $7.00 because Saudi Arabia suddenly decided to quit being the swing producer maintaining the high price of oil. The Saudis wanted the other OPEC members to cut back on their production to help sustain the $34 price. The others said they would, but actually did not. So the Saudi's who had cut their production to dangerously low levels in sustaining that price, decided to up their own production and let the market decide the price. The sudden collapse in oil prices caught all the major forecasters off guard: they had forecast a more or less continuous price rise for the next several years, not precipitous collapse.

Shock number five was the sudden collapse of the Soviet Union. Most Kremlin watchers (including Henry Kissinger) never doubted that Russian communism would endure . . . right up to the day the USSR collapsed in August 1991.

One result of this string of forecasting failures was an almost simultaneous rejection by American top management of the notion that powerful computers enabled economists to make accurate forecasts. Only fools, many top managers began saying, could believe such nonsense. The trouble was, the folks in finance did not get the word, as we shall shortly see.

Economists themselves hardly let those shocks and failed forecasts dissuade them. They stuck with their linear world of false assumptions in which they had an enormous vested intellectual interest. Business managers, however, were heavy users of those economic forecasts. By 1985 they saw they had been sold a bill of goods on the forecasting power of mainframe computers. American corporations fired over two-thirds of their economists. In Seattle where I lived at the time, every last economist in every Seattle bank was sacked. The Seattle First National Bank went bankrupt (though subsequently rescued by Bank of America) trusting their economists' claims of ever rising oil prices. Bill Jenkins, the CEO, issued orders to lend multi-millions to oil-well wildcatters based on those forecasts. When oil prices collapsed, the wildcatters promptly went bust, walked away from their loans, handed over their now worthless drilling equipment and left Seafirst insolvent.

Boeing had already let go of all their economists in 1982 except for yours truly. I survived in part because by then I had become an increasingly vocal critic of the mainstream theories. I had also warned that based on historical precedents, oil prices could collapse. They soon did. But, again, academic economists sailed along without much concern, wed as ever to their linear way of thinking, ever unwilling to rethink any of their major assumptions.

So here we come at long last to the logic of the Black and Scholes equation. It became a basis for claiming that linear mathematics could largely rid us of risk in leveraged speculation. Again, however, let us be clear: neither of these two gentlemen bears any responsibility for creating the conditions that caused this intellectual environment in economics. They were simply being as creative as they could within that environment. They were both brilliant men working within that well-accepted paradigm. Moreover, the formula worked in individual cases within limits. It failed when it became the norm and everyone jumped aboard. Individuals could pass the risk on but the risk was still out there.

THE BLACK AND SCHOLES OPTION PRICING FORMULA

Fischer Black and Myron Scholes created the formula below that aimed to price an option to buy a particular stock on a particular day in the future, and took account of the price movement of the stock during the intervening period. They concluded the value, C, of the option depended on five variables:

1) S = the current price of the stock
2) X = the future price at which the option could be exercised
3) T = the expiration date of the option
4) r = the risk-free return in the economy as a whole (often taken as the rate on a 30-year U.S. Treasury Bond)
5) σ [the Greek lower-case letter sigma] = the expected annual volatility (price fluctuations) of its price between the time of purchase and the expiration date of the option

Taking all this into account they deduced the value, C, of the option to the following formula:

$$C = SN(d_1) - Xe^{-rT}N(d_2)$$

where

$$d_1 = \frac{\log\left(\frac{S}{X}\right) + \left(\tau + \frac{\sigma^2}{2}\right)T}{\sigma\sqrt{T}} \text{ and } d_2 = d_1 - \sigma\sqrt{T}$$

If you feel somewhat intimidated by all this, rest assured, most of us do. That is why many economists call it a "black box."

Even many economists and finance managers would, at first sight of Black and Scholes's equation, either read right past it or shut the book. That was just fine with the folks who could read the equation, understand it, and then act upon it. They were suddenly the enlightened ones. These high priests of finance were now in possession of a new and crucial secret of the financial temple. That secret insulated them—the ones in the know—from those prudes calling for the money-changers to be thrown out of the temple. This time it was different because risk had been taken care of by the black box of Black and Scholes. The money-changers had now become the high priests of the temple. If you followed their advice these priestly and sophisticated money-changers could make you rich and do it quick. By all means let us keep them around and celebrate their virtues. The lay world soon celebrated them as financial geniuses who now gave greed their divine blessing. Yes!!! Greed is good.

Here we come to a major cross current of economics and business. By 1990, American operating management had taken a decisive turn away from the old linear and mechanistic model. In good part influenced by Japan and Dr. Deming's part in their quality success, many corporations began embracing teamwork, team spirit, and a new respect for labor. But the finance folks, those in Wall Street and even in many corporations were not really buying in. They wanted to stick with the old ways because the new ideas presented by Black and Scholes made it rewarding to do so. They believed that mathematics, wed to powerful computers, would eliminate the risk of leverage. And while innovations in computer technology and its software were coming fast and furious, so were innovations in ever more sophisticated financial derivatives and debt instruments. These lent themselves to leveraged speculation and were enormously successful in converting American savings into debt.

Deming's ideas helped the manufacturing sector recover quickly from its 1980 low point. Quality improved sharply, and hoards of irrelevant staff planners were redeployed as a wave of antibureaucratic re-engineering programs took place. Teamwork became a new mantra and employees all over the country were no longer "hired hands"; they suddenly became "associates." Real progress was made . . . that is up to about the year 2000. But in various ways both subtly and overtly, those clever folks on Wall Street—whose predecessors helped engineer 1929—were laying the groundwork for 2008, either blocking or even undoing much of the real, recent progress in quality, better customer service, and in work-place human relations, all, of course, to create more shareholder value. What the operations folks had been constructing, the Wall Street financiers, in cooperation with corporate bean counters, began deconstructing, and with a vengeance. They could not see beyond accounting numbers. They could not really get it that satisfied customers were the best way to earn profits and the best way to get satisfied customers was to motivate employees to work with that satisfaction in mind. They saw employees not as instruments of profit creation, but as costs to be got rid of.

Thus Wall Street financiers were perfectly happy considering employees as impersonal hirelings to be hired and fired at will. They liked the ethic of the "economic man" because it enabled their greed, while partners would likely pose a constraint on their greed. That Wall Street ethic justified their taking over healthy companies, hollowing them out, dismantling and selling off the parts with nary an afterthought of the effect on morale, management continuity, the local community, product or service quality, or simply on people's lives. Wall Street often breaks out in cheers when, after a takeover, the acquiring firm sacks thousands of the employees. Make no mistake, neo-classical economics fully justifies such hip-hip-hooray thinking. So what was it to be? The exploitation of labor in the interests of enriching financial capital? Or a corporate partnership between capital and labor that constrains greed and shares the fruits of free enterprise in an equitable way between the two stakeholders and makes customer satisfaction a major goal for both partners?

By about 2000, the lure of greed had clearly won the day. Suddenly, corporate CEOs could see the prospect of bonuses rising from, say, half a million dollars or so to hundreds of millions of dollars, even if the company lost money, and especially after they had laid off workers by the thousands. Enron has become a prime example of this ethic of greed. In the end, such greed drove Dr. W. Edwards Deming's ethic of customer service, product quality, teamwork, esprit de corps, and shared rewards right out the door. Subconsciously, mainstream economists felt relieved. By holding on to a discredited eighteenth century theory, no matter what its problems, academic economists could count on Wall Street for enormous intellectual support, and more directly, for jobs. So the academicians, with a deeply vested interest in it, no longer felt much pressure to revise a theory that justified greed. Black and Scholes's extended thesis of risk-free leveraged speculation had swept aside Deming's challenge. They could continue to look for new ways to use leverage to get rich quick. We will dig deeper into this and related issues again in Chapter 3.

But here is a truly sad outcome. From the average professor's viewpoint, his or her vested interest in the neoclassical model is not personal wealth. *They simply want to be able to teach economics as if it were a branch of linear mathematics.* Thus when those professors pose test questions to their students, they can demand and expect to get precise numerical answers. For example, how many more angels will dance on the head of a pin if the price of pins drops by 10 percent?

So now let us turn to the financial deregulation that began in 1980. Black and Scholes's thesis that the risk of leverage could be much reduced became the strongest intellectual support for financial deregulation. Deregulation began just as Dr. Deming's quality revolution appeared on the scene. This revolution arose from bottom-up teamwork actively pursuing total quality management in order to put the customer first and provide fair shares for all who achieved that goal. The two visions clashed, and greed soon got the upper hand.

NOTES

1. Wallace, William McDonald. "The Great Depression Reconsidered: Implications for Today." *Contemporary Economic Policy* 13, no. 2 (April 1995) pp. 1–15.

2. Taylor, F. W. *Principles of Scientific Management.* 1909.

3. Wallace, William McDonald. *Postmodern Management: The Emerging Partnership between Employees and Stockholders.* Westport: Quorum-Greenwood, 1998. Note: when I wrote this book, Glass-Steagall had not yet been repealed, and it was not then clear to me why the financial sector was happy with the adversarial relationship.

4. Gleick, James. *Chaos: The Making of a New Science.* New York: Viking, 1987. The first chapter describes the butterfly effect and how it came to be discovered.

Chapter 2

FINANCIAL DEREGULATION
OF THE EARLY EIGHTIES

Hardly anyone outside Wall Street had heard of Black and Scholes until quite recently. Yet these two gentlemen played a major role in getting financial deregulation accepted. Congress had put comprehensive controls on the financial sector during the Great Depression following Wall Street's 1929 crash. It recognized that leveraged speculation, by making it easier to get rich quick playing the market, dangerously amplified greed while injecting much greater risk into the system. That lust too often trumped rational behavior. When the lust for wealth powered explosive trading, asset prices escalated beyond reason, creating a bubble that was bound to burst. And when it did, it would wipe out all the new-gained wealth but leave behind the debt that had financed the speculation. In the hindsight of the thirties, it was clear that once a bubble starts, it is politically very difficult to control. If the Fed pushes up the rate of interest or otherwise constrains credit, prices stop rising and that is all it takes to pop the bubble. Few politicians or central bankers want to be responsible for blasting investors' hopes. Thus Central bankers waffle and tend to let the bubbles keep going until they burst, but always hoping they will not.

The trick is to prevent bubbles from starting in the first place. The best way to do that is to make it difficult to speculate with borrowed money, or else to place a heavy tax on such transactions. Bubbles rarely form when people speculate with their own money. But politicians often welcome bubbles in their early stages because they give off an illusion of prosperity, the sense of a rising tide that will lift all boats. Politicians are eager to take credit for such "prosperity" and often do. Of course, nothing more encourages such early irrational exuberance than a *laissez-faire* conviction that the government should under all circumstances let the free market do its own thing. And clearly, without the freedom of competition that *laissez-faire* entails, the high tech modern world could never have evolved. Lacking such freedom, the entire ancient world on all continents saw very little innovation arise until after the fall of Rome, and then only in Western Europe where a new freedom to innovate arose following the end of central control from Rome.[1]

Unconstrained freedom, however, can give license to addictive greed, to a lust to get rich quick that can generate bubbles that must ultimately burst. All competitive sports need rules of engagement to control competition and thus avoid competitive self-destruction. So does speculation. Speculation can perform a real economic service, but only if it remains rational and within reasonable bounds. Rational speculation occurs when speculators use their own money. Irrational and excessive speculation often emerges when investors can speculate on credit—using other people's money (OPM). You could say OPM is the opiate of the investing, or speculating class.

By 1980, thanks to Black and Scholes, it seemed that we could now use sophisticated mathematics wed to powerful computers to greatly reduce the risk of speculating in the stock market. In the context of the times this seemed to be a plausible conclusion. In business, engineering and in government, computers were allowing us to do things we could never do before. Certainly the idea that computers would allow us to minimize the risk of leveraged speculation was coherent with McNamara's quantitative approach to management at that time. As mentioned earlier, a widespread feeling had arisen by 1980 that the web of regulation had gotten too pervasive, too complicated, and at times, contradictory. And 45 years after the Great Crash, many of its lessons had been forgotten. Most of the players of 1929 had passed from the scene, taking their personal memories with them. And it was not just finance that cried out for deregulation. Much resentment centered on the overregulation of the shipping and transportation industry—railroads, trucks, buses, and airlines. By the late sixties, for an airline to get a new fare authorized or a new route implemented meant jumping through a frustrating and expensive nightmare of bureaucratic hoops. Such regulation seemed to yield little more than paralysis through never-ending analysis.

On the financial scene some of the Depression-era regulations had clearly gotten out of sync with other changes that took place. Consider the Savings and Loan Banks, often called the thrifts. They, along with FHA (Federal Housing Administration) Fannie Mae and Freddie Mac, had been created as "chosen instruments" to make and service home mortgages. The Federal Reserve Board had been given authority under Regulation Q to regulate the interest rates paid to depositors and the rates charged for mortgages. The Fed allowed the thrifts to pay out a slightly higher rate on savings deposits to encourage savers to put their money into the thrifts. That edge assured the thrifts sufficient funds to lend out for mortgages—the only kind of loan they were allowed to make. For many years this made for a very stable situation. One wag called it the 3-6-3 system. The thrift paid depositors 3 percent, charged 6 percent on the mortgage loan, and by 3:00 p.m. the bank president was out on the golf links.

This very stable system, however, was disrupted during the Vietnam War. President Kennedy had convinced Congress to make cuts in marginal income tax rates in 1963, shortly before his assassination. But soon after, in 1965, we began to get heavily involved in the Vietnam War. (And war, with few exceptions, introduces inflationary pressure into the economy.) The Fed asked President Johnson to convince Congress to repeal Kennedy's tax cuts as a way to curb consumer spending, and thereby prevent inflation. But President Johnson refused; he felt support for the war was tenuous at best and he did not want to further alienate the taxpayers. The Fed responded that since their job was to prevent inflation, they would have to raise interest rates in lieu of higher taxes in order to damp down demand. This was a significant change in itself, since interest rates had remained stable for 30 years.

As the Fed raised interest rates, the money market rates on such things as certificates of deposit rose correspondingly. Soon enough, many savers began pulling their funds out of the thrifts to get the higher rates. As deposits drained out of the thrifts, the funds available for mortgage loans dried up, and many of the thrifts had to stop making mortgage loans. When the thrifts quit lending, new housing starts plunged. That in turn triggered higher unemployment rates among the construction workers. Needless to say, all the parties involved here were extremely unhappy.

To add insult to injury, however, the higher rates did not in fact curb inflation, and indeed, were not even needed. Demand persisted because the higher rates spurred lenders to relax credit terms to borrowers in order to reap the full benefit of the elevated rates. The Fed would have been more successful simply tightening up on the terms of credit—as they had done earlier, during the Korean War. That conflict started on June 25, 1950. With memories of the Second World War still fresh in their minds, consumers were immediately fearful that it was the beginning of World War III and that military requirements would sharply cut the supply of consumer goods. Anxious buyers stoked demand and prices at once began to rise, especially for major items such as automobiles and appliances. In response, the Fed imposed a rule of 30 percent down and 15 months to pay. Inflation promptly fell from 10 percent to 2 percent, and the Fed was able to keep the prime rate at 1.5 percent, as it had been for 13 straight years.

In 1965, the argument against control of credit terms was that the Fed really had no business interfering with the free operation of the market. But what about interfering with the market by raising interest rates, which caused housing starts to crash, followed by massive layoffs of construction workers?

As it happened, the conventional, monetarist, wisdom of the time prevailed: The Fed had to use interest rate adjustments to curb inflation. To avoid the stop/go consequences of a policy of tight regulation, the call went out for deregulation of the thrifts. The thrifts would now be able to match market rates on deposits, lend in areas other than real estate, go into the credit card business, and in general "let freedom ring." If the Feds put up interest rates to curb inflation, the thrifts would now be able to create competitive money market instruments on their own, yet still continue lending on mortgages. Their business became much more exciting than it had been under the 3-6-3 system. But it also became much more dangerous.

As below, so above. When teenage boys are released from the constraints of parental authority and go off on their own with new found freedom ringing in their ears, a certain percentage are sure to go wild and crash. That group often includes teenagers who were quite well behaved while under parental constraints. Something similar happened to the thrifts after deregulation. Once free of the Fed's constraints, they really cut loose. They began to compete fiercely with each other, making new loans at high rates. And they crashed by the score. It was the old story of bubbles that burst, or at least a variation of it, driven by the same lust. The Fed (that is the taxpayers) got stuck with a huge bailout bill as hundreds of thrifts went under.

But let us look at this more broadly. It is a fact that as it evolves, life will exploit every opportunity to grow and expand until stopped. If grass seeds, for example, are spread on fertile ground the grass will at once begin to grow and spread new seeds until the grass has exploited all the fertile ground or is otherwise stopped. If put on an island containing lush plants suitable for browsing, deer, in the absence of any predators, will browse, reproduce, and rapidly increase their numbers. At some point however, the growing deer population will have eaten the entire available browse. Suddenly without food, a massive die off of deer inevitably follows.

Easter Island is a famous example of primitive humans who destroyed their own habitat and society by expanding until stopped by the very destruction their expansion created. They might as well have had the brains of deer. But they had human brains, and they put them to work in a difficult engineering project erecting great monoliths all over their island—the sight of which is now the island's chief claim to fame. It seems the population broke into competing segments, each trying to outdo the other in erecting the most monoliths. To move the huge stones, however, they needed rollers, and these they cleverly fashioned out of the trunks of trees. But the more stones, the more trees were chopped down until they had cut down all their trees. Easter Island became windblown; the seabirds left, the inhabitants no longer had wood for their fishing canoes, etc. The population of the original settlers was about 60. Over the next few hundred years the population rose to over 10,000 and then crashed and fell to about 1,000 by the time the first European ships arrived in the eighteenth century. Food had become so scarce they turned to cannibalism.[2]

Freedom, in short, is a double-edged sword. It is evolution's great arena of trial and error. For humans, the emergence of the high tech modern world reflected a series of highly successful technological trials, starting with the printing press and followed by steam and steel, railroads and automobiles, airplanes, rockets, computers, the World Wide Web and much else. But the evolution of the modern world has been dotted with plenty of errors along the way . . . a record of boom and bust. Freedom can bring out the best and the worst in us, the booms and the busts. Freedom reigns during the boom but is again constrained following the bust.

Deregulation of the Savings and Loans, or thrifts, brought the first big bust of the new *laissez-faire* period. It began almost at once. But it is also true that such deregulation brought forth many changes that were highly popular, as, for example, easy access to revolving credit with bank cards such as Visa and Master Card. Deregulation allowed the thrifts to enter the revolving credit market and they did so in droves. Here, again, however we confront our double-edged sword. An explosion of consumer debt began at once thanks to revolving credit that never requires a down payment and never actually requires pay off, providing you make the interest payments. Revolving credit made it simple for consumers to leverage their standard of living well beyond what their income would allow on a pay as you go basis.[3]

And leverage their consumption they did. Big-box stores proliferated, and new retail space expanded rapidly as consumers financed their spending with easy credit. It appears the spending went well beyond needs: with garages filled to overflowing, a whole new consumer warehouse industry sprang up to provide the storage space for excess stuff. Those storage places hardly existed before 1980, then grew like mad until about 2007.

OPM in the form of revolving credit had become the opiate of the consumer masses, creating an explosion of consumer debt that played an important part in the 2008 meltdown. For years, consumers had been spending beyond their means, and it finally caught up with them. Today they are cutting back, and as they do, scads of retail space has gone vacant all over the nation.

Traditionally, America's Puritan ethic urged people to work hard, avoid luxurious living, and save, save, save. Borrowing money was okay to start or expand a business. Such loans were made to earn the money to repay the loan and hopefully yield a profit. But it was considered imprudent to borrow money in order to live beyond one's means with the possible exception of a home and later on, a new automobile in order to commute to work. Yes, stores often let people run charge accounts, but these were normally to be repaid in full after payday at the end of each month. Credit cards, such as gasoline cards, department store cards, American Express, or Diner's Club were also to be repaid at the end of each month. These were convenience cards, again to be paid in full every month.

America's high philosophical and ethical regard for savings, however, took a severe blow in the Depression thanks to John Maynard Keynes. Keynes in effect argued that too much saving and too little spending by the rich helped cause the Depression.[4] Savings had long been needed to create the investment funds that power a modern industrial economy. But in the thirties, President Roosevelt had put down that wisdom in a blunt way by saying, "Our industrial plant is built." Therefore, one could argue, saving was no longer so important and perhaps even harmful. Spending became the new watchword because now that our "industrial plant was built," it was limping along at about only 60 percent of capacity and millions were out of work. Saving took on overtones of personal selfishness while spending became the socially responsible thing to do, even when consumption meant going into debt. The macroeconomy was now seen to be driven by consumer spending augmented by deficit spending by the government.

To sum up, financial deregulation became acceptable for a number of reasons. First, it was justified by the frustration of overregulation. Not only conservatives, but also many liberals became aware that the government could and often did overregulate in harmful ways. Second, the clearly demonstrated dangers of leveraged speculation in the 1929 crash were often forgotten 40-odd years later. Third, the rise of Keynesian macroeconomics provided legitimacy for consumer spending and debt that in turn created a background climate for marginalizing consumer saving. Fourth, the classical economic theory of *laissez-faire* created a background climate that seemed to support the notion that greed is good, the argument being that the drive to "get rich quick" keeps the economy growing. Fifth, the long legacy of Darwin's uniformitarianism had, for over 100 years, cut economic theory off from seeing the process of evolution as it actually takes place. Evolution of all life is not uniform; it is a process of punctuated periods of change followed by long periods of stable equilibrium. Boom and bust in many variations plays a major role in the punctuated periods of evolution where chaotic changes arise. A valid theory of economics, micro or macro, needs to take such chaos into account and, as of now, none does. Further, a valid theory needs to recognize, as none now does, that economic equilibrium *must* constrain chaos and competition. That constraint, however, must not limit too severely the personal freedom upon which innovation and economic growth depends.

So, having seen why financial deregulation came about, let us turn in Chapter 3 to the revived philosophy of *laissez-faire*. We will see how it embeds the argument that greed is good. We will look at the limited extent to which greed performs a service, but focus on the much larger arena where it does great harm, once leverage pushes it out of control.

NOTES

1. Wallace, William McDonald. *Techno-Cultural Evolution: Cycles of Creation and Conflict*. Dulles, VA: Potomac Books, 2006. Chapters 11 and 12 document the fall of Rome and the revival of innovation thereafter.

2. Diamond, Jared. *Collapse: How Societies Choose to Fail or Succeed*. New York: Viking/Penguin, 2005. See also Ehrlich, Paul. *Human Nature: Genes, Culture, and the Human Prospect*. Middlesex, England: Penguin, 2002. Both these books give excellent accounts of the fate of Easter Island's crash following overexploitation.

3. Nearly all the books published recently on the 2008 collapse make this point. Two good ones are: Ferguson, Niall. *The Ascent of Money: A Financial History of the World*. New York: Penguin, 2008 and Elliott, Larry and Dan Atkinson. *The Gods That Failed: How Blind Faith in Markets Has Cost Us Our Future*. Nation Books, 2009.

4. Keynes, John Maynard. *The General Theory of Employment Interest and Money*. McMillan, 1936. Nearly all modern macroeconomists made the same point. Keynesian-based textbooks coined the term "the fallacy of composition."

Chapter 3

THE RETURN OF *LAISSEZ-FAIRE* AND THE RECELEBRATION OF GREED

The concept of economic man (homo economicus), formulated in the early days of the classical economic model, claimed that greed has a socially useful outcome. Crudely put, the lust for money energizes innovators and entrepreneurs to get going and produce goods and services that we all need. Personal greed equals social utility, so to speak. Adam Smith reflected this view in his famous statement, "Not out of altruism do the butcher, the baker, and the brewer create the food for your dinner, but in order to make their own living."[1] Stated that way, Smith's claim is more or less true. In the process of taking care of ourselves, we accommodate the needs of others as well. Altruism is not always necessary to serve others (but at times it surely helps). Still, taking care of ourselves hardly equates to greed, nor does it preclude altruism toward others.

But legitimate or not, the "greed is good" argument went into deep hiding after the Crash of 1929. As the Depression unfolded, there suddenly came to light colossal examples of greed during the "roaring twenties." Some of the scoundrels had claimed their greed served "broader social interests." Even the true believers blanched at that one, and for years thereafter they more or less kept quiet. It was nearly 50 years before "greed is good" resurfaced as a serious argument. It was famously expressed in the 1987 movie *Wall Street* by Mike Douglas's character, Gordon Gekko, in a speech to insurance executives: "The point is, ladies and gentlemen, greed, for lack of a better word, is good. Greed is right. Greed works." (Douglas won an Oscar for his portrayal.)

Given the free competition of *laissez-faire*, moreover, logic suggests that greed does indeed have its place. The greedy tend to compete more fiercely and thus are more likely to win and survive. (Nice guys finish last, as cynics often say.) Thus, from the point of view of evolution, one can defend greed when it enhances success defined as survival. But at the same time, we should also note that, when greed runs wild, it can also cripple success. The events leading up to the 2008 meltdown clearly demonstrate that fact. In the first decade of the twenty-first century, greed was literally running wild, not so much in the streets perhaps, but on Wall Street certainly, and in many a corporate board room, such as at Enron, for example.

Bank officials, hedge fund managers, mortgage brokers, and others were pocketing multi-million dollar bonuses even while wrecking their firms. It was literally an orgy of greed.[2]

As a conservative, I was shocked that many fellow conservatives tended to defend such nonsense as "market driven." I suppose one could say a drunken barroom brawl was "market-driven" and therefore okay. Certainly a barroom brawl could be used as an example of unconstrained *laissez-faire*. Still, standing aside a bit, our twenty-first century Wall Street orgy appears to be a clear example of the overexploitation of opportunity that leads to a crash. It was the O before C in FROCA (Frontier, Release, Overexploited Opportunity, Crash, and finally Adaptation).[3]

It could be said that *laissez-faire* was a god that failed in 1929. But it can also be said that faith in government regulation to promote the public welfare had come to a similar if less dramatic fate by 1980. As Charles Morris put it: "Liberal cycles inevitably succumb to the corruptions of power, conservative cycles to the corruptions of money."[4]

Let us drill down a bit into the evolutionary reasons why people so often overdo a good thing and thus ruin it. If tycoons got carried away with greed in the last decade or so, so regulators got carried away with their power to control others. Regulation, as with most processes, is subject to the law of diminishing returns. Too little regulation and one risks competitive chaos. But too much regulation often brings about operational rigidity, even paralysis. Rules tend to become ends in themselves and get detached from the problem they were designed to prevent. If conditions have changed since the time of a rule's inception, a "letter of the law" application of the rule can even make things worse. Bureaucratic organizations have a tendency to keep regulating well past the point of diminishing returns. Again, we deal with some truths of evolution here. Even as all life tends to expand until stopped, all life also attempts to remain self-consistent in the face of an ever fluctuating local environment. Put another way, all life tries to behave in a way that is true to its nature. Biologists have called this tendency "autopoiesis," a term coined from Greek that roughly translates as "self-making."[5]

In a bureaucracy if one is given the job of rule making, one continues to make rules even when new rules pass the point of diminishing returns. Thus legislators legislate, legislate, and keep on legislating. They tend to make laws ever more complex, difficult to follow, difficult to understand, and often contradictory. To illustrate: Buying a home 25 years ago may have required five or six pages of documentation. Today it is likely to require 50 or 60 pages. But the folks who make such rules and laws are simply being self-consistent, doing what their very identity requires. They behave in the way their innate life force commands them to behave *for their given identity*. Again, autopoiesis drives us here. It is much like the law of self-preservation, only now preserving the individual identity, rather than the physical organism per se. As such, it guides human social and economic behavior in our day-to-day life in ways still poorly understood—and utterly ignored by economists.

America's culture is built around a philosophy of individualism and personal rights. These values helped create the modern high tech world based on an explosion of innovations. These values are also woven into our personal identities and we take great pride in them. Moreover, these values strongly support personal ambition and justify the striving for personal wealth gained through competitive endeavor. Competing against others and trying to win is a fine and noble thing to do in our culture. But in cultures more driven by the desire to preserve traditions that are in themselves deemed sacred, the value of personal ambition is often suspect.

Calvinism and its Puritan work ethic also fit comfortably with individualism and its web of values. While this web can be used to justify greed, Calvinism acts as a strong brake on greed because the Puritan ethic prefers plain living and takes a dim view of luxury and ostentation. It also strongly supports savings. Calvinism urges us to work hard in our calling and live a plain, pious, frugal, and self-reliant life with God as its central focus. It was the German sociologist Max Weber who first proposed this connection between Calvinism and the rise of capitalism in his most famous book, *The Protestant Ethic and the Spirit of Capitalism.* Though written early in the twentieth century, Weber's book was translated into English by Talcott Parsons only after World War II. It became a big hit in business schools at the time. I personally devoured it because Weber seemed to provide an indirect answer to a big puzzle in my mind when I entered graduate school. As I said in the Preface, when I returned to Japan in 1954 during a sixteen month tour of duty in the Far East, mostly in Korea, I was astounded at the progress the country had made in the six years since I had first visited it as a crew member on an Army transport ship in 1948. It seemed then Japan would not soon recover from the physical devastation of the war. The progress I saw triggered in me a broader question, as I mentioned earlier, about the causes and sources of Japan's dynamism.

Max Weber's book on the Protestant ethic alerted me to the fact that a business can have a spiritual dynamic of its own, a fact that none of my economics courses had ever so much as suggested. If Northern Europe could create capitalism out of a feudal agricultural background, why not Japan? True, Japan was not Protestant or even Christian, but Japan did have its hard-hitting samurai warrior code. I soon learned that many of Japan's largest business firms had been founded by samurai, beginning with Mitsui in the early 1600s.[6]

By this time (1957), Keynesian economics had seized the academic high ground and Keynesians, led by Paul Samuelson, largely dismissed Weber's work. They rejected the idea of a spiritual dynamic that could drive economies. For them, it was all a question of input-output analysis, investment levels, and their multiplier effects, etc.

Keynesian economics, meanwhile, had marginalized the Puritan sanctity of savings. Instead, it celebrated consumer spending, and the mostly liberal majority of economists simply were not willing to concede any validity to a spiritual dimension in economic activity; in their view it was so much "mystical crap." The Keynesians shared Robert McNamara's philosophy of positivism, still riding high at the time, that if you couldn't put numbers on it, then it didn't count. This focus on numbers to the exclusion of nonmaterial, or spiritual values is a major force behind the misconceptions that underlie 2008. In more tradition-directed societies social obligations and nonmaterial values take precedence over personal rights. Greed still might get the best of individuals, but that behavior brings shame, not social approval.

Japan was clearly a tradition-directed society where social obligations trumped personal ambition. Thus Japan's ethic of economic growth made little room for personal rights or individualism. When Japan began seriously to industrialize after the 1868 Meiji Restoration, seeking personal gain had little to do with it. Instead, Japan was determined to preserve "the spirit of Japan." That goal required that Japan avoid becoming a colonial dependency of America or of the European powers as had the Dutch East Indies, large parts of China, India, Burma, and the Philippines. Being pragmatists, the Japanese saw that to preserve their political independence and thus their "spirit," Japan had to match Western technology and its weapons. By 1868 it was also clear that such technology, for example battleships, could be had only by industrial powers that could make the steel, the engines, the artillery, and all else that went with it. But as it happened, Japan had a rigorously enforced caste system topped by the samurai warriors, followed by farmers, artisans, merchants, and last by the untouchables, those people relegated to do "spiritually unclean work" such as butchering animals, tanning leather, etc. But in a move that startled all Europeans and Americans, the Japanese promptly ditched the caste system in the interests of preserving Japan's broader spirit. They saw—quite clearly in fact—that a caste system would seriously interfere with industrialization, so caste had to go.

Japan offers us outstanding illustrations of autopoiesis-in-action on both the macro and micro level, which is to say on both the community and individual level. For example, we can learn the different ways in which American and Japanese cultures handle personal ambition versus an individual's sense of obligation to the community with which he or she identifies. In America, with a few exceptions, personal ambition takes precedence over community obligations, and that fact gives America an advantage when it comes to innovation. In Japan, again with a few exceptions, a sense of obligation to the greater community trumps personal ambition. That fact made preserving the spirit of Japan of supreme importance to the individual soldier in World War II. That sense of personal identity with the Japanese spirit played a big role in motivating the kamikaze suicide pilots in that war. It accounts for the fact that, in battle after battle, Japanese soldiers continued to fight to the death well after it was clear they could not possibly win. That behavior played out on Tarawa, the Marshalls, Saipan, Guam, Iwo Jima, and finally on Okinawa when it was clear beyond any doubt that Japan had lost all hope of winning.

In other words, defeated soldiers chose physical death to preserve Japan's spirit. To them, thanks to autopoiesis, preserving their larger spiritual identity seemed superior to merely prolonging the life of the physical self. As individuals we all physically die in the end, but Japan's soldiers could assume their spiritual identity would survive forever if they died to preserve that broader spirit. They also assumed that even if Japan lost the war, honoring their code of Bushido by dying in a lost cause would prove the sincerity of the cause and therefore help preserve its spirit.

While American troops often felt in awe of Bushido behavior, they wanted no part of it personally. In fact most Americans felt that the Japanese needlessly squandered thousands of troops in their futile banzai attacks. American troops saw no shame in giving up when all hope was gone. Those who surrendered on Bataan and Corregidor were thought heroes. No one expected them to squander their lives when out of food, hopelessly cut off from supplies, and with no possibility of relief.

American troops also took pride and gained confidence from the fact that their country would spend awesome sums on search and rescue missions, often just to save one stranded American pilot. That is something the Japanese never did.

The first President George Bush was the pilot of a torpedo bomber shot down off Chichi Jima in 1945, in sight of the Japanese, who were shooting at him. Bush was rescued by an American submarine that had been stationed offshore for just that purpose. Years later President Bush returned to that island and from a hillside pointed out to Japanese veterans from the island where he had been rescued. One of the Japanese veterans in the Bush party had himself witnessed Bush's rescue. He went on to say that Japanese who observed the rescue gained some insight into why Japan's ethic to fight to the death never came close to breaking American morale as it was supposed to do. He went on to say the Japanese knew their country would never do as much to rescue their pilots and thus gained respect for America's different approach.[7]

I cite these wartime differences because they help explain the differences between the Japanese and American approaches to business organization and the way each side views its economy.

We may note, in passing, that the differing attitudes of American and Japanese soldiers stand out all the more clearly since the two countries' organization of their military services was almost identical. (Both Japan and the United States owed much, in fact, to the influence of the early Prussian General Staff that created the framework for nearly all modern armies.) For example, in Japan and the United States, the army and navy each had its own air force. Germany and Britain, however, had an independent branch, the Luftwaffe and the Royal Air Force, respectively. In America and Japan the army divisions were organized much the same way into regiments, battalions, companies, platoons, and squads. Military rank was about the same. In both Japan and America, the military was a focal point of patriotism, and members of the armed forces were loyal members of their branch of service, not impersonal hirelings.

When we turn to examine the role of rank and file workers in both countries in the postwar period though, we find a different situation. In the United States, workers were viewed as impersonal hirelings and not members of the firm. The Japanese, however, considered workers members of their firm, partners in an extended corporate family where loyalty was as important a value as in the military. Songs such as *Anchors Aweigh* or the Marine Hymn were sung in the military services of both Japan and America. Significantly, many Japanese companies have equivalent hymns, but such songs are a rare occurrence indeed in American corporate life. I make these comparisons to clear up a misconception. The relevance of Japan's famed industrial teamwork is often discounted by American economists. They cite Japan's admittedly homogenous culture as the major reason for that teamwork, thus making it irrelevant to us. According to this argument, the Japanese learn respect for authority, group cooperation, and loyalty on their mother's knee. They are taught to suppress the individual ego in the service of these values. American economists compare that upbringing in Japan to the American situation: a heterogeneous country made up of a wide range of ethnic groups, races, and creeds, many of whom hate each other. Moreover, America adheres to a philosophy of individualism that does not put the group ahead of the individual. All this is largely a matter of fact.

But those facts do not explain the different behaviors of American versus Japanese workers. Moreover, it cannot explain the often superb morale, dedicated sense of loyalty, and outstanding teamwork in American military units such as the Marines. Supposedly, our culture of individualism precludes such behavior. Yet economists know perfectly well that our culture does in fact permit and often encourage such behavior. So why do economists hide from the evidence Japan provides? I suspect the tradition that comes out of classical and neoclassical economics based on the asocial economic man gives economists a fine perspective from which to dismiss Japan's different approach, and thereby avoid cognitive dissonance.

We can see a similar situation in Great Britain. Professor C. Northcote Parkinson, who studied British organizational behavior and authored *Parkinson's Law* in 1954, was challenged by a puzzling situation. Why, he asked rather plaintively in the sixties, did Britain's Royal Marines exhibit remarkable loyalty, fully respect their superiors, and perform to as high a standard of excellence as any in the world, while the Queen's own royal coal miners were a disgruntled lot who hated their bosses, engaged in "go-slows," and would strike at the slightest excuse? After all, Parkinson observed, the coal miners and the enlisted men of the Royal Marines are recruited from precisely the same (largely white) working class group of young men. Their deportment, however, could hardly be more different. The answer—and the point I want to make here—is that the specific culture and social order of an organization has much more influence on the behavior of its members than does the broader culture. The circumstances of employment of the Royal Marines and the "royal" coal miners are revealingly quite different. Miners are hirelings; Marines are members of their service. The Marines provide a clear path of promotion as one gains experience and skill. For the miners, there is no such thing. Furthermore, the miners' loyalty is divided by competitive claims, first from the state as the employer and second, from the miners' trade union as protector against a predatory state employer. The union usually has the prior claim.

Similar differences exist between corporate American workforce and the military. Before going into those differences, however, I want to compare Japanese and American military teamwork during World War II. I do this, once again, to refute economists' contentions that Japan's culture much more effectively molds its citizens to act as team players than does America's much more individualistic and multi-ethnic culture. What is true is that organic organizations are much more effective at achieving teamwork than are mechanistic (primarily bureaucratic) organizations. That is true regardless of whether the broader culture is group centered or focuses on individualism.

Since World War II, many people fear the term "organic" because both fascists and communists used the term the "organic state" as an excuse to create a closed society that tyrannized individuals who disagreed with their policies. The individual was supposed to focus only on the state to which total loyalty was owed, and in preference to family, friends, or business ties. By that definition, one might even have applied the label to Japan before World War II. Since the war, however, a democratic Japan has clearly shown that the "organic firm" based on a partnership between capital and labor has distinct operational advantages over its mechanistic Anglo-American counterparts that feature an adversarial relationship.

Meanwhile, America's democracy has always used an organic approach to the military, and with outstanding results, from the outset of World War II on. The U.S. standards of air combat teamwork during the war still remain the envy of the world. In such team-centered tactics as the "Thatch Weave" or the "Delmonico Mowing Machine," American naval fighter pilots—even in inferior planes at first—outperformed Japan's pilots, who seemed to emulate lone feudal samurai warriors. The Americans, with outstanding teamwork, bested the Japanese by a lopsided margin.

In the corporate world, though, we see a reverse picture. What the American military did with teamwork in World War II, the Japanese have done with industrial teamwork in the postwar period. In both cases, the teamwork took place within an organic format, meaning that the team players were members of their organizations and not impersonal hirelings. Here again autopoiesis suggests an explanation. Organic organizations convey personal identity in quite different ways from the traditional mechanistic way. A member of an organic organization has a personal rank that attaches directly to him or her. That rank conveys both a pay rate and relative status. It does not normally define the job. Secure by personal ranks in status and pay, the organic members then more likely identify with the whole organization, not their job and department. They are much less resistant to redeployment since such moves do not normally impact status and pay secured by personal ranks.

In the mechanistic organization the impersonal job defines both the pay rate and the relative status of the incumbent. It seems perfectly normal to pay the job and not the person doing the job, a relationship that fits nicely into both the classical and neoclassical model. After all, a company hires people to do a job. Moreover, jobs clearly vary in their relative importance, so what could be more natural than to create a hierarchy of jobs that reflects the relative importance of each job—and pay the holders of those jobs accordingly. It all fits into the commodity theory of labor inherent in the classical and neoclassical model based on the impersonal buyer-seller relationship.

That whole set of relationships, however, means that autopoiesis will drive jobholders to be extremely defensive about their jobs if they are a vital part of their life. From that fact stem many other consequences that, for the most part, economists largely ignore. I have described these consequences in depth in my book, *Postmodern Management* (see note 3, p. 51). Let me summarize those consequences here. First, as noted, is the dysfunction of job defensiveness. Bureaucracies the world around, and quite apart from local cultural values, are job defensive, much more so than organic organizations. Second, and related to the first, job holders tend to suboptimize their jobs and departments, not the whole organization. After all, the organization virtually forces them to identify with the part—their job—and not whole. Third, since status and pay are tied to jobs, the promotion ladder is largely a case of rising up in job rank. Now, to be socially acceptable, a promotion ladder needs to have many rungs so lower level employees see a way to rise up in the system. But, to be efficient, a chain of command needs to be short to avoid miscommunication up and down. So, when the chain of command is the promotion ladder, the two requirements are in direct conflict.

As a practical matter, the imperative of the promotion ladder usually wins out by the tactic of creating more levels and more jobs than efficient management requires. Needless links in an elongated chain of command lead directly to over-staffing, the fourth dysfunction. And over-staffing, among other things, leads to a fifth major dysfunction, namely the proliferation of regulations and rules that hinder performance. Such red tape also requires labor-intensive management and yet more personnel to monitor for compliance. Job defensiveness, suboptimizing, overlayering, overstaffing, and red tape are dysfunctions typically found in bureaucracies the world over. In virtually all cultures, as a result of this common set of dysfunctions, the word bureaucracy has pejorative implications. (Even Mao Zedong condemned bureaucracy in his *Little Red Book*.) It should be noted these dysfunctions apply equally to private and public organizations whenever bureaucratic employment policies are in force.

Again, let me stress that frustration over these dysfunctions of control played a major role in motivating the 1980 wave of financial deregulations. The old Marxist idea that employees working for a publicly owned operation would perform selflessly on behalf of the "people" had since become a joke. Bureaucrats, it was by then well understood on the street, perform mainly in their own self-interest.

We mentioned in Chapter 2 that American management began to recognize the advantages of organic organization at about the same time that financial deregulation began to take place. We also mentioned these two trends also began to conflict with each other by about 2000. We saw that continued deregulation won. The vision of getting rich quick trumped the tendency to improve the management of American companies. As it turns out, management greed is well served by a policy of using hired labor instead of organic partners. Hirelings are paid simply to do a job. They therefore do not share in the profits or in the capital gains. They have no say in leveraged buyouts. They cannot prevent a company from being bought out and dismantled. On the other hand, in the interests of "shareholder value," hirelings can be fired by the thousands or "let go" when their factories are shut down and their jobs shipped overseas. All such meat-ax decisions are justified on the grounds of enhancing shareholder value. But, as some have pointed out, the hirelings who lost their jobs may also have benefited by "enhanced shareholder value" in the stocks in their 401k plans . . . except that after 2008, those funds suddenly became "201k" plans. Many lost their jobs *and* retirement nest eggs at the same time as shareholder value went into the toilet. They now had to live on unemployment compensation and scrambled nest eggs. This was too high a price to pay to cling to the myth of economic man.

Though conservatives are generally clear about the importance of family values outside the economic arena, conservative philosophy has always handicapped itself by its inability to get real about social values and interactions within the economic arena. (The idea of treating capital and labor as natural partners instead of adversaries never got through to conservatives.) Until I woke up to the fact that partnership placed a big constraint on the untrammeled greed of capitalists, I could not understand why. Those obscene bonus payments, however, woke me up. After Stan O'Neal walked away from Merrill Lynch with about 150 million dollars in exchange for bankrupting the company, though, I understood.)

Similarly, I could not understand why liberals, long the friends of labor, did not themselves propose partnership between capital and labor. Then it occurred to me. By doing away with the adversarial relationship upon which unions depend, a partnership between capital and labor could render unions irrelevant. Supporting the idea of such a partnership, then, could cost liberals the political support of trade unions. In addition, liberals would also lose a traditional cause prompting their quest for political power. Ironically, I concluded, the myth of *homo economicus* turned out to serve very well the quite different hidden agendas of both liberals and conservatives. Capitalists needed economic man to serve their greed and liberals needed him to justify their pursuit of political power. The one needed him in the form of faceless hirelings, the other in the guise of hapless victims of capitalist exploitation. Neither one had any use for a harmonious partnership between capital and labor.

Thus, liberals did not seriously challenge the return of *laissez-faire* with its risk of letting loose an orgy of leveraged speculation and greed. Even so, it is the conservatives who must, in the end, accept the main responsibility for deregulation. If they could celebrate the growth and wealth that post-1980 *laissez-faire* bubbles seemed to create, then conservatives must also accept responsibility for the meltdown that followed when those bubbles finally burst. Too many conservatives are still in denial that *laissez-faire* was also a god that failed, once again, just as it had in 1929. The Marxist god of communism seemed to offer a better solution than free enterprise in the 1930s. But the Marxist god also failed, and disastrously, in 1991 when the USSR collapsed in an implosion. But all is not lost.

Free enterprise is not a god that failed. Economic man failed. Let me end by pointing out some "made in USA" examples of my point. At the end of World War II, two companies were launched in the Midwest. In Bentonville, Arkansas, Sam Walton created Walmart. In St. Louis, Jack Taylor began a new car rental business, Enterprise Car Rental. As do many new companies, both began as family enterprises. Both treated their employees well. Both began with a creative new business plan and avoided head-on competition with more powerful competitors. Enterprise catered to auto repair shops providing vehicles to customers whose cars were being fixed. For years, you never saw Enterprise outlets at airports. For its part, Walmart aimed at small towns below the radar of the giants like Sears or K-Mart. For years, Walmart avoided the big cities where they knew they would be at a competitive disadvantage. Walmart also aimed to offer customers the lowest possible prices. To do that, they became creative with new electronic technology. When scanners were developed Walmart used them to control inventory in a novel way. The store began to record the sale of products and sent the data to the suppliers. Procter & Gamble's Pampers was the first product tracked like this, I believe. In this way, the company or its supplier would then know just when to resupply the store in question, and they would do so automatically. This process saved Walmart a bundle on inventory costs. These savings were promptly passed on to the customer, giving Walmart stores a big competitive advantage in their local areas. As the company expanded, Walmart developed a superbly efficient supply chain management system and ultimately became the largest retailer and employer on the face of the earth.[8]

Enterprise Car Rental did not put electronic technology to work in a new way, but it maintained its belief in teamwork. Indeed the company takes its very name from World War II's most famous aircraft carrier, the USS *Enterprise*, upon which the founder served during the war. That carrier was the main ship on which the Thatch Weave, the Navy's famous aerial combat tactic already mentioned, was developed and tested at the battle of Midway Its creator, Lt. Thatch, proved that, by relying on teamwork, pairs of relatively clumsy Wildcat fighters could beat off the far more nimble and faster Japanese Zero fighter planes.

In any event, when Jack Taylor began Enterprise Car Rental, he was certain that he could use superior teamwork to successfully challenge his better-financed and much larger rivals such as Avis and Hertz. He knew that superior teamwork came from self-motivation inspired by more than just an impersonal exchange of work for money. But he also realized that such motivation would require that the team players receive their fair share of the revenue. Having seen it work in the Navy, he was convinced that a culture of loyalty, esprit de corps or camaraderie was needed to sustain good teamwork dedicated to customer service. To this day, the morale at Enterprise Car Rentals seems very high. Customer service is imbued in most employees, and that is possible because they share fairly in the rewards. At Saint Martin's University, some colleagues and I studied the Enterprise culture in the Seattle area. One thing in particular leaped out at me. Enterprise was thoroughly integrated with respect to race, gender, etc. But the company had developed a culture that encouraged all employees to focus on customer service and to take great pride in it. One could sense the high esprit de corps. It was totally different from Walmart.

Now one suspects that Sam Walton was more or less sympathetic to family-like feeling, judging by the early years of his company. But following the deaths of the founders of the two companies, Walmart and Enterprise began to evolve in quite distinctive ways in terms of their respective cultures. After the death of Jack Taylor, Enterprise remained a family operation and set up policies explicitly to institutionalize a family-like feeling. They adopted, without any reference whatever to Japan, the Policy Priority of (1) Take care of the customer first. (2) Take care of the employees second to make sure they will put the customer first. (3) Do those two things first, and the profits will come to the stockholders. Following the death of Sam Walton, however, Walmart rather quickly morphed into the more typical bureaucratic company with a pattern of employee relations where the workers are regarded as impersonal hirelings. Morale began to sink. Employees felt no passion of loyalty to the firm, convinced that Walmart felt no such passion toward them. Thanks to the superb efficiency of the supply chain management, Walmart continued to enjoy great financial success and continued to drive weaker competitors out of the business. However, Walmart's post-Sam reversion to the practice of impersonal hirelings so beloved by Wall Street and most economists cost them heavily in terms of good will. As Walmart drove inefficient local firms out of business, they became villains in the eyes of many. That reputation in good part arose because Walmart failed to create a loyal workforce sticking up for their company. After all, there is something good to be said for Walmart. It has brought down the cost of living by perhaps 25 percent to folks who must live on welfare, unemployment, or minimum wage. Yet, despite that, Walmart is one of the more disliked companies in America, even to the extent that Hillary Clinton's service on their board was considered a negative during her Presidential bid.

Yet another homegrown example of how bringing employees into a partner-like sense of employment pays off is Lincoln Electric. The firm was founded early in the twentieth century by John Lincoln, an engineer, to market an electric motor he had invented. He soon discovered he didn't like dealing with the business side, and asked his brother, James, to take that over. James Lincoln had little experience in managing people, but he knew the only way it would work was if he had the loyalty of the work force. So he surveyed the workers and asked what they hoped to get out of working for Lincoln. They responded with two big hopes, namely job security and participation in profits. James Lincoln thought for a moment and decided that was pretty much what he wanted as well.

Without going into detail, James created a compensation plan that consisted of three parts, a fixed base rate, a personal productivity bonus, and a bonus that reflected the corporate results. With that system, James Lincoln imparted flexible labor costs to such a degree that he could implement a no layoff policy. It worked. Lincoln quickly became the most efficient manufacturer of arc welders and their peripheral equipment in the world. Their workers became among the highest-paid blue-collar workers in America by end of World War II. They have remained in that category. James Lincoln was clear on policy. The customer is first, the employees come second, and if that order is preserved, profits will come. But putting profit first is apt to undermine the first two objectives and lead to losses, not profits. The surprising thing is this: Lincoln Electric is a perennial subject for case studies in business schools, as I discovered about 1958. Yet none of my professors suggested it was a model for the future. They all applauded Lincoln Electric, but then went on to explain why it wouldn't work generally. Having just discovered the Japanese had been doing something similar on a large scale, I just could not understand why economists were so negative about that organic model.

So, to repeat: free enterprise has not failed us. Economic man failed us in 2008 just as he had done in 1929. He justifies greed, whether via the exploitation of labor at work or as lust for getting rich quick via leveraged speculation. We need only reject the concept of economic man and his adversarial relationship and replace it with some form of real partnership between capital and labor. If we do that with labor, we will have pulled the philosophical rug out from under the justification of greed via leveraged speculation run wild. Neither liberals nor conservatives have gotten that message, but maybe 2008 will help both to do so.

NOTES

1. Smith, Adam. *An Inquiry into the Nature and Causes of the Wealth of Nation*. London: Ward, Lock, and Bowden & Co., 1776. Smith's book has been continuously in print since its first publication.

2. Faber, David. *And Then the Roof Caved In: How Wall Street's Greed and Stupidity Brought Capitalism to Its Knees*. John Wiley & Sons, 2009. Faber gives an excellent and detailed account of the subprime mortgage bubble based on 20 years as a senior reporter for CNBC.

3. Wallace, William McDonald. *Techno-Cultural Evolution: Cycles of Creation and Conflict*. Dulles, VA: Potomac Books, 2006. Chapter 1 gives a full description of the FROCA process.

4. Morris, Charles. *The Two Trillion Dollar Meltdown*. Public Affairs Books, 2009. p. xxiii.

5. Wheatley, Margaret. *Leadership and the New Science: Discovering Order in a Chaotic World*, 2nd ed. San Francisco: Berrett and Koehler, 1999. pp. 20, 40. See also Capra, Fritjof. *The Web of Life: A New Scientific Understanding of Living Systems*. San Francisco: Anchor Books, 1996.

6. Wallace, William McDonald. *Cultural Values and Economic Development: A Case Study of Japan*. The University of Washington, 1963.

7. Bradley, James. *Flyboys: A True Story of Courage*. Boston: Little, Brown & Co., 2004. Bradley relates this story of President George H. W. Bush as one of several such accounts in his book.

8. Friedman, Thomas J. *The Earth Is Flat: A Brief History of the 21st Century*. New York: Picador, 2007.

Chapter 4

THE LOGIC OF FINANCIAL BUBBLES THAT BURST

Financial bubbles almost always burst, and they almost always arise from three causes: leverage, debt, and greed. The leverage is created by borrowing money to bet on some future outcome. Leverage amplifies the power of a small amount of your own money to make a much greater profit than is possible from just your own funds. For example, suppose you buy a $300,000 property with a 5 percent down payment that comes to $15,000. Suppose that a year later the market value of that property has risen by 10 percent and is now $330,000. Your profit is not 10 percent, it is 200 percent because you only had $15,000 of your own money invested. But after the price has gone up 10 percent, you have equity of $45,000 ($15,000 from your original investment plus $30,000 profit) and thus your profit is now twice as much as your original investment. Now that is nice.

Suddenly your greed kicks in, amplifying your lust for leveraging your own money with other people's money. Like the drug opium, using OPM to get rich quick suffuses one with a sense of euphoria when the bet pays off. You soon become hooked. Moreover, and better than opium, you feel energized by a new excitement. As your winnings mount, it is oh so good to be alive. You are very proud of the shrewdness of your investments. You look forward to profits that shrewd investors such as you rightly earn. You feel an enormous release from the financial constraints of your past. Again you owe it to the sharpness of your investment decisions. (You easily dismiss the fact that, in the past, nearly every big, leveraged bull market collapsed sooner or later. You wave off such negativity by insisting "this time it's different.")

Alas, you have entered the unreal world of Alan Greenspan's "irrational exuberance." Greed is, of course, a natural human emotion and has its uses. For one, it limits the ability of others to take advantage of us. However, most social orders use peer pressure to constrain greed and keep it within normal bounds. If, for example, we try to grab more than our share of food at dinner, our dining companions usually put us down. Their greed cancels ours. Early in life most people learn to restrain their own greed. We do that in order to retain the goodwill of others. Being social animals, good will is vital to our own sense of social well-being.

Unfortunately when policy allows and even encourages leveraged speculation, the inhibiting peer pressure tends to vanish. Instead of peer pressure, we enjoy the admiration of others when our leveraged investments pay off. We can even become celebrated financial icons when we make it big, as did George Soros after successfully speculating against the British pound sterling. We all love a winner. And there are many while the market is going up. But like soap bubbles, it is in the nature of leveraged market bubbles to burst. Euphoria suddenly becomes terror, greed becomes fear. What others yesterday hailed as our shrewdness, they now condemn as stupidity. How could we have been blind to the fact that speculative bubbles always burst, and when they do, great damage occurs?

The collapse of 2008 is a good macroeconomic example of the damage caused when we create policies that dissolve peer pressure and make it easy for greed to seem good rather than bad, which is just what happens when leveraged speculation—betting with other people's money—is condoned.

In short, bubbles arise because monetary policy and financial regulation allow them to. Such policies are usually justified by the theory of *laissez-faire*. History shows that such hands-off policies on leverage all but assure that bubbles will arise, and when they do, they will just as inevitably burst. Alan Greenspan himself was clear that once a bubble forms, it cannot be stopped by the action of the Federal Reserve Board. That is, unless the Fed constrains credit in a way to assure that the bubble does burst. Once a bubble forms, one must remember, it will continue to expand only if ample credit for speculation is available. If the Fed constrains that credit, the bubble must burst.

It may be a good thing to cause the bubble to burst sooner rather than later. But what official in a democracy would have the strength of character to take that step, given the harm to perhaps millions of people that would follow (not to mention the criticism)? It will hardly mollify those people who lose everything for the Fed chairman to say, "Well, if I had not caused that bubble to burst now, a bigger burst would have hurt even more people later."

So Fed chairmen in the past have usually done little more than hope the free market will take care of the problem. After all that is what free markets are supposed to do under *laissez-faire*. And of course, the market will take care of the problem sooner or later: One day the bubble will burst seemingly on its own, driven by the logic and the psychology of the "irrational exuberance" that arises in the absence of normal peer pressure to restrain greed. Now *laissez-faire* assumes that people behave rationally in their own best interests, and indeed, they often do just that. But Greenspan's own choice of words, "irrational exuberance," suggests that when people get caught up in leveraged speculation, they abandon their rational thinking and behavior before they enter the marketplace.

Here let us clearly distinguish the effect of a financial bubble that bursts from a boom that goes bust. The difference is leverage. If you own an asset free and clear, whether stock, bonds, real estate, or whatever and the price drops, you still own the asset. Say you have assets with a market value of $1 million and the market falls by 20 percent. Your assets are now valued at only $800,000. Your boom has gone bust. You have suffered a "paper loss" of $200,000 on the value of the asset, but you still own the asset.

But now suppose you leverage your $1 million by a factor of 10 and use that money to buy $10 million worth of assets. If the price goes up, say by 12 percent, you have more than doubled your money and your net worth is now $2.2 million. But suppose the price drops by 12 percent and the broker calls and says he needs that other 2 percent to maintain those assets. Say you cannot raise the cash. Your broker then sells you out and you are now broke. Not only are you broke, you still owe the difference between what you borrowed to buy the asset and what the broker could sell it for. In a down market the price may have fallen by another 10 percent before he could sell, and so you are not only broke you now owe $1.2 million. In this case, your bubble has burst. You have lost your $1 million asset *and* you are now seriously in debt.

None of this is really new; bursting bubbles as we now understand them go back nearly 400 years. The first modern bubble was the huge rise in future contracts to buy Dutch tulip bulbs. The Dutch first acquired tulip bulbs from the Ottoman Turks. Serious cultivation began in Holland in 1593 and by about 1630 tulip bulbs had become very popular as a form of investment. According to Wikipedia "In 1636, the Dutch created a type of formal futures markets where contracts to buy bulbs at the end of the season were bought and sold." Prices shot up astronomically and in 1636 one investor claimed to have made 60,000 guilders in four months. (The annual salary of the mayor of Amsterdam was 500 guilders.) In February of 1637 the tulip bulb market collapsed. In 1841, Charles Mackay, a Scottish journalist, published the first extensive account of Dutch tulip mania in a book entitled *Extraordinary Popular Delusions and the Madness of Crowds*. It has been quoted extensively ever since.

Beginning about 1980, just when *laissez-faire* was making its comeback, proponents of the efficient market hypothesis (EMH) began to downplay the Dutch tulip mania, even claiming it was not a real bubble. Professor Earl A. Thompson of UCLA claimed the huge 1636 price increase followed by a collapse was a rational response to changes in contractual obligations, stating that "Tulip contract prices before, during, and after the 'tulip mania' provide a remarkable illustration of 'market efficiency.' " (Thompson wrote this in 2007.) In the early eighties, Jude Wanniski, a former editor of the *Wall Street Journal*, made a similar claim about the price of common stocks before and after the crash of 1929. No matter how much irrational exuberance the market displayed, it was deemed rational by those enamored of *laissez-faire*. Any market outcome was a rational outcome according to those skilled in such rationalizations. When *laissez-faire* began reemerging as a respectable philosophy around 1980, its promoters seemed to feel they had to cleanse history of any speculative bubbles. The bubbles had to be transformed into rational responses to unusual market situations. In fact that is what the efficient market hypothesis (EMH) must do. If real bubbles can and do form, then the efficient market hypothesis is false.

In their book *The Gods That Failed*, Larry Elliott and Dan Atkinson noted that bubbles and other speculative rampages seem to go through distinct phases. The first phase often begins with a change in the economic climate as a result of financial innovations. It the case of tulip mania it was the introduction of futures contracts in early 1636. Asset prices, in this case, tulip bulbs, naturally rose as a result: More demand often results in a higher price. In the second phase, other investors see an opportunity and jump in. Again prices rise in response to higher demand. In the tulip mania instance, it was investors outside of Holland who wanted to speculate in tulip bulbs. In the third phase, "irrational exuberance" begins to take over as rising prices convince many investors that they will always be able to sell at a higher price than they paid. Exuberance and the hope of getting rich quick displace reason. The final phase of course is a collapse in the price. In the case of tulip mania, the peak occurred sometime between December 1636 and early February 1637 when, suddenly, tightening credit and prices literally beyond reason, no one was willing to buy any more. Fear and panic replaced hope and greed. In a matter of days, people who owned bulbs found they were worth barely a fraction of what they had paid for them, while those who held contracts to buy bulbs discovered they would be paying many times more than the collapsed price bulbs were now fetching.

Similarly, in 1719, the Mississippi bubble arose in France after the creation of a central bank and the issuing of paper money (both innovations introduced by John Law) dramatically facilitated trading in shares. Much the same thing happened again with England's South Seas bubble in 1720. As Elliot and Atkinson point out:

> Financial markets are endlessly innovative, always coming up with new money making ideas. The public is eternally credulous, suspicious only in the aftermath of a crash, but soon convinced by those tulips, railroad shares, shares in dot-com stock, or real estate, "that this time it's different." (*The Gods That Failed*, p. x)

Elliot and Atkinson go on to note that *"this time it's different"* are the five most dangerous words in the lexicon of markets.

True, but such cynicism leaves out the fact that financial innovations are not the only innovations that count. In the last 150 years, new and often startling technology innovations preceded the financial innovations and in fact made them possible. The existence of these new technologies made it much easier to argue that this time it really was different. Consider the Wall Street Crash of 1929. The big rise in common stock prices is often said to have begun when stock brokerage firms first, went national, and then second, offered to sell common stocks to investors on margin, in this case at 10 percent down. Brokers could only introduce these innovations once the new technology of the telephone had been extended to form a network covering the whole nation, and the technology of the stock ticker tape made it possible for all investors to get real time stock price quotes everywhere at the same time. So the stock market in the twenties was indeed different because of new technology as well as financial innovation. And though such differences did not change the underlying logic of "irrational exuberance," they did make it much easier to ignore past experience.

The South Sea bubble of 1720 originated with the innovation of converting government debt into equity in the South Sea Company in exchange for a monopoly on trade with South America. This innovation truly did seem different: it appeared to make the company a guaranteed money-making machine. And inevitably, irrational exuberance followed. Elliot and Atkinson quote Adam Anderson's 1764 history of the South Sea bubble as follows: "The unaccountable frenzy in stocks and projects of the year 1720 may by some be thought to have taken up too much room in this work; but we are persuaded that others of superior judgment will approve . . . as a warning to after ages."

Not really. Many commentators made similar comments after the Great Crash of 1929. Meanwhile, as was the case with the Mississippi and South Sea bubbles, the Great Crash revealed all sorts of corruption in its aftermath. The collapse of the dot-com boom brought similar revelations. Alan Greenspan would testify in Congress as follows: "At the root was the rapid enlargement of the stock market capitalization in the latter part of the 1990s that arguably engendered an outsize increase in the opportunities for avarice. Our historical guardians of financial information were overwhelmed." But Greenspan then went on to claim the situation had been put right and everything in the financial sector was again okay: "Perhaps the recent breakdown of protective barriers resulting from a once-in-a-generation frenzy of speculation is now over. With profitable opportunities for malfeasance markedly diminished, far fewer questionable practices are likely to be in the immediate future" (Testimony given before the Senate committee on Banking, Housing, and Urban Affairs on July 16, 2002).

In point of fact, serious malfeasance was really just getting started, fostered in part by that very Senate committee. (I have in mind the subprime mortgage crisis, about which more later.) Regardless, Greenspan's "once in a generation" comment was just plain wrong. Before the dot-com boom and bust there was the savings and loan fiasco in the 1980s that came almost immediately after financial deregulation. Then came the stock market crash of 1987, which occurred following the financial innovation of Black and Scholes—that is to say, of their theory that clever hedging, guided by complicated mathematics processed on mainframe computers, enables investors to avoid such busts. Ironically, it was that very theory that brought the market down, because when everybody takes advantage of a clever idea, it ceases to be clever. In this case, it actually caused and then accelerated the 1987 collapse, although, as Michael Lewis points out in his book, *Panic* (Norton, 2008), Alan Greenspan moved quickly and contained the bust so well no real recession followed.

Irrational exuberance, however, is not limited only to leveraged speculation. Jim Collins organizes his recent book, *How the Mighty Fall* (HarperCollins, 2008), around five stages. First, we see the hubris born of success. Humans have been doing this as far back as recorded history goes. Second comes the undisciplined pursuit of more—irrational exuberance if you will. Stage Three, according to Collins, is the denial of risk and peril, common across a wide spectrum of society from criminals to addicts of almost any kind, and of course to leveraged speculators. Stage Four begins after the peril becomes real and cuts through denial and people begin grasping for salvation. That failing, we enter Stage Five, where people begin to give in to their fate, even to the point of welcoming death, perhaps through suicide. Collins goes on to point out these stages are not deterministic. They are strong tendencies but we can avoid them if we want to, and his book suggests ways of doing so.

The best way to avoid the irrational exuberance that financial bubbles elicit has already been proven. It was clearly demonstrated between the crash of 1929 and the savings and loan fiasco of the early eighties: simply prohibit strong leveraged speculation. An alternative solution would be to limit the tax on capital gains to a tax on leveraged gains only, but why do it indirectly in a way that tempts people to game the system? We need access to credit at reasonable interest rates. And it is also true that speculation on future values serves a useful purpose. But to speculate with other people's money on the future value of anything is unnecessary and dangerous.

Chapter 5

MIGHTY BUBBLES FROM LITTLE ACORNS GROW

The Association of Community Organizations for Reform Now (ACORN) was not the only element in the formation of the subprime bubble. But it did play a key role by focusing on racial prejudice in redlining. Beginning in the 1930s, banks in many cities had begun to identify and "redline" certain areas which they considered too risky to invest in—neighborhoods where they refused to make real estate loans. Blacks and other minorities such as Hispanics were often the main residents of redlined neighborhoods. Starting in the 1960s, activists in such communities began to insist they had been redlined only because of race.

Of course race was not the only relevant variable. Income levels, credit record, net worth, outstanding debt, and employment history all enter into the question of whether or not to make a mortgage loan. The redlined areas usually had a substandard record on all these counts. Yet in many cases the only variable that got much publicity was race or ethnic difference. That suggested, quite falsely, that all the other variables were satisfactory. Considering only the race variable, there were clear differences as to who did and who did not get loans. For example, in his recent book,[1] Thomas Sowell presents interesting data from a Federal Reserve Board study. For conventional mortgages the approval rate for whites was 76 percent and for blacks 56 percent. However, whites also scored better on all the other variables relevant to approving or disapproving a loan: credit record, net worth, and employment history. Moreover, as Sowell points out, Asian Americans had better credit scores and enjoyed higher loan approval rates than whites. Does that data prove that banks discriminate against whites? Hardly, but it does show banks consider credit records, etc. as more important than race.

Another example. The *Atlanta Journal Constitution*[2] published the following statistics regarding subprime credit rating scores for different groups in the Atlanta metropolitan area: Asians 10 percent, whites 16 percent, Hispanics 34 percent, and blacks 52 percent. Percentages for subprime mortgages roughly paralleled the credit score data. But in the controversy over redlining, such data were almost always either ignored or suppressed. The media, sometimes even conservative media, often fail to mention different credit score data when citing the different rates of approval by racial or ethnic category. This is somewhat akin to a prosecuting attorney withholding evidence that the defendant was not at the crime scene when a murder was committed.

Still, before 1960, racism was widely practiced even if it was also criticized. No doubt creditworthy people were denied loans as a result. By the late sixties, however, overt racism was largely illegal and had become unacceptable in most parts of the culture and indeed, was viewed as a major social sin. But, even as more and more racist practices became illegal, many civil rights activists continued to insist *covert* racism was still widespread and getting worse. (Merely being accused of covert racism strikes fear into the hearts of business managers. No one can prove they are innocent; negatives simply cannot be proved as a matter of principle.) And some federal agencies, despite the documented differences between the races on credit ratings, ruled that statistical differences between the races in rates of lending approval were *prima facie* evidence of racism and those banks could be, and sometimes were, punished accordingly.

The *Los Angeles Times* reported one instance where the banks found themselves burdened by the new federal statutes:

> ACORN, for example has used the CRA (Community Reinvestment Act of 1977) as leverage to compel banks to create pools of loans for low and moderate income families. Its efforts have generated about $6 billion in loans to these borrowers while also generating funds for ACORN's non-profit housing corporation. Supporters say this is a win-win scenario; critics claim it is legalized extortion.[3]

One critic claiming "legalized extortion" was Republican Congressman Paul Broun of Georgia, who said that the banks in his district "couldn't expand their services or put in ATM machines unless they would make these bad loans." On the other hand, Democratic Congressman Barney Frank of Massachusetts defended ACORN and its efforts because, he claimed, activists were merely "trying very hard to preserve some equity and social justice" and were "people whose only crime was to offend powerful political interests because they [presumably the activists] cared about equity."[4]

Because of such pressures, many banks did relax their terms of credit to allow minority applicants with a bad average credit history to qualify for mortgage loans. Once that new credit ethic was in place, it became much easier for anyone with a bad credit history to get a subprime loan and before long "deadbeats" were lining up for subprime loans, as Thomas Sowell has pointed out.

Now liberals such as Barney Frank can make a very good case that the financial deregulation of 1980 was a major cause of our 2008 crash. They rightly claim a need for governwent regulation of the financial sector. I agree on both counts. The financial sector, in fact, depends for its very existence on government to insure the enforcement of laws concerning contracts, the limited liability of corporations, and much else. The case for regulation is clear.

But liberals often fall woefully short of acknowledging their own role (in Frank's case major, highly visible, and well documented) in using government intervention in the housing market to impose their social engineering goals such as "affordable housing." Liberals have also militantly ignored their part in the major defaults in the financial industry that were direct consequences. Nevertheless, Frank makes it clear he feels that those who resist his liberal vision, however well based their resistance, should indeed be punished. The fact is that financial deregulation by itself could not have brought about the subprime mortgage bubble that began to crash in late 2006 and (hopefully) hit a bottom in the autumn of 2008. It was first necessary to destroy a long history of sound credit standards. That destruction opened the floodgates of leverage to speculators in the housing market. It also invited people to take home mortgages who could not possibly afford to repay the money borrowed. Bad credit records, spotty employment histories, low incomes, and no assets were no longer barriers to getting a loan. Borrowers need not even provide cash for their own closing costs—they were just rolled into the mortgage.

Attorney General Janet Reno gave lenders a clear warning when she said that the Justice Department would "closely examine their lending practices and take necessary measures to eliminate discrimination." In many cases, as economist Paul Craig Roberts made clear, "Believe it or not, there were no individual complaints [of discrimination] from minorities. All that was necessary was a statistical difference in loans by race *and in the absence of taking account of credit records, employment records, or income.* Banks could even come under fire simply for not having opened up a branch in a "minority neighborhood."[5]

But there was also another well-intended liberal intervention in the housing market. It too played a big role leading up to the 2008 collapse of the subprime bubble. Starting about 1970 some parts of the nation began imposing severe building restrictions in the interest of "growth management," preserving green space, curbing urban sprawl, and preserving farm land for future generations. All these goals were well intended. On their own merits, a good case can be made for any or all of them. But there were to be serious unintended collateral consequences, some of which were obvious. From the end of World War II until 1970, U.S. housing prices had risen at the rate of inflation more or less evenly across the whole nation. After 1970, real estate prices began rising much faster than inflation in precisely those areas where severe building and development restrictions were imposed. California's coastal regions had the biggest rise while sharp price increases also took place elsewhere in the Southwest, Florida, New York City, and the Washington DC area. Analysis quickly confirmed that the difference was almost entirely in the cost of real estate, not the buildings. There were some prosperous population centers such as Houston and Dallas in Texas that had imposed few new restrictions on land use, and real estate prices there continued rising at about the general rate of inflation, much as they had been before.[6]

The different rates of housing price increases were shocking. By 2006, a four-bedroom house with two and a half baths in Dallas or Houston cost about $155,000. In the San Francisco area, however, the price for the same house was about $1 million. Silicon Valley, just south of San Francisco, became noted for its million dollar hovels. One result of the big run up in housing prices was that poor people were increasingly driven out of these markets which they could no longer afford. In many cases, poor still meant disproportionately minority populations. So, for example, the percentage of blacks in San Francisco by 2006 had fallen by 50 percent compared to 1970, according to Thomas Sowell. Similarly, "between the 1990 and 2000 census, four California counties—Los Angeles County, San Mateo County, Alameda County, as well as San Francisco County, have had their black populations fall by more than ten thousand each, despite increases in the general population."[7]

Yet such collateral consequences did not fit the prevailing environmental vision, and so were widely ignored. Meanwhile, the record of trying to improve things by the construction of public housing in poor neighborhoods has had a dreadful record. Such housing projects often become centers of drug trafficking, gang wars, and other crimes so bad the police are reluctant to patrol them. The so-called section eight housing program—subsidizing the cost of housing for the poor to live in affluent neighborhoods—has fared little better because of sharply clashing behavioral standards of say, ghetto cultures, compared to affluent middle-class communities.

The shift in vision to lift up the poor by allowing them to get subprime mortgages was an even worse disaster because the damage it caused spread far beyond the ranks of the poor, contributing to a global financial collapse that has hurt everyone. This could not have happened without financial deregulation to be sure, but deregulation as such was not enough. It was also necessary that government laws and regulations both directly and indirectly foster the elimination of sound credit standards intended to prevent just such debacles of default. ACORN was not the only participant in that process to be sure, but it did play a vital role in getting that process of "social engineering" started.

We see here a long-established tendency by both liberals and conservatives to ignore the realities of human behavior in favor of the idealized behaviors of their respective ideologies. Conservative ideology insists people are always rational in their economic decisions. Liberal ideology argues that individual misbehavior results mainly from "social injustice." And liberals then go on to suppose that removing the social conditions that cause misbehavior will enable people to behave rationally. The overwhelming evidence from the real world—including the startling 2008 meltdown—proves both propositions are dead wrong. It is of course true on the conservative side that some people do often, perhaps even most of the time, behave rationally in their economic decisions. But, it is also true that irrational behavior is not at all rare, indeed it can become all too common given conditions of unconstrained leverage.

On the liberal side it is true that social injustice can lead to misbehavior. But it is equally true that people can and do misbehave even when they enjoy conditions of social justice. Moreover, remove all credit standards in the name of social justice and you guarantee massive misbehavior by borrowers and lenders alike. After the subprime mortgage bubble burst in 2007–2008, the forces of political correctness made a strong effort to absolve ACORN from any responsibility. Oh sure, ACORN may have made a few mistakes and employed a few bad apples . . . what large organization doesn't? . . . ACORN was only doing its job. By the fall of 2009, however, all sorts of other misbehavior made the news such as ACORN offering clear advice on how to get a prostitution ring going using sub-teen immigrant girls. It also came out that the founder's brother stole several million dollars from the organization and was not even disciplined. Many ACORN employees have been convicted of fraudulent voter registration and thousands of those registrations had to be thrown out in several past elections, as many news reports in the autumn of 2009 revealed.

Let us turn next to the politics of both the dysfunctional practices as they came together to produce the subprime mortgage bubble. Let us examine in greater detail just how both liberals and conservatives got it wrong.

NOTES

1. Sowell, Thomas. *The Housing Boom and Bust*. New York: Basic Books, 2009, pp. 99–101.

2. *Atlanta Journal-Constitution*, "Black Atlantans Frequently Snared by Subprime Loans," Section B-1. April 26, 2007.

3. *Los Angeles Times*, "Don't Blame the Victims," Section A-22, October 25, 2008.

4. *Washington Times*, Column, "How to Rob a Bank Legally," December 20, 1993.

5. Janet Reno quoted in: *Washington Times*, "Bank to Pay $960,000 in Loan—Bias Settlement," Section A-2, December 14, 1993.

6. Sowell, *Housing Boom and Bust*, Chapter One.

7. Ibid., p. 108.

Chapter 6

A Faustian Bargain: How Liberals and Conservatives Both Got It Wrong

Nearly everyone reacted with shock to the crash of 2008. Many of us expected a correction, but not a crash on the scale that took place. Both liberals and conservatives, however, were quick to blame the misguided philosophies of the other. Of course, both philosophies have long tended to demonize each other. What was new this time was that in the period leading up to the 2008 subprime bubble collapse, each camp made a sort of Faustian bargain with the devil to gain practical acceptance for their own demon within. As it happened, the devil each camp bargained with was the other's demon. This bargain was of course informal and unspoken. Still the deal was that liberals would tolerate the conservative demon of leveraged speculation with other people's money if the conservatives would go along with the liberal demon of demolishing credit standards for home mortgages to provide affordable housing for the poor. Of course to conservatives, their demon appeared to them as the angel of freedom of economic action. And liberals saw their demon as the angel that showered compassion on the downtrodden. Neither side expected that this bargain would backfire, but when it did, and with such force in 2008, both sides promptly blamed the other's demon.

A quote from Elliot and Atkinson could well and truly apply to both. They imagine economists and others surveying the crash of 2008, this way:

> They will resemble gatherings of liberal school masters who, bewildered by the destructive consequences of having allowed the kids to express themselves, wring their hands as they survey the devastation, unwilling to contemplate the admission that they were horribly, utterly wrong.[1]

For conservatives "the kids" were the leveraged investors speculating with other people's money under their philosophy of *laissez-faire*. The "free expression" for these "kids" was supposed to unleash the wealth-creating powers that free markets motivate. For liberals "the kids" were subprime mortgage homebuyers and the investors who bought up bundles of those toxic mortgages. Give the poor access to affordable housing and it would transform them went the liberal view. But to achieve that social goal, credit standards had to be virtually abolished. Liberals consoled themselves by arguing those standards were simply racist. Those credit standards, many liberals insisted, aimed mainly to deny the "deserving poor" and especially poor minorities, from gaining access to the middle class. After all, liberals could claim, ACORN had "proved" as much.

Both liberals and conservatives clearly saw the other's philosophy as toxic. Conservatives saw that defaults would skyrocket if credit standards were virtually abolished. Liberals were clear that "free expression" by leveraged speculators would lead to bubbles. But both sides denied that their own philosophy was also toxic. In the event, it took both toxins acting in concert to produce the double-demon devastation that resulted when each of those demons began freely to "express itself." Under the traditional home mortgage credit standards that conservatives backed, real estate investors would have had little leverage in the home market. Housing could not have become a global bubble had credit standards been tight. Given the constraints liberals favored against the demon of leveraged speculation, investors could not have speculated on house prices with other people's money to nearly the extent they did. But even with leveraged speculation on house prices, no bubble could have formed had not the conservatives gone along with the liberal demon that abolished sane credit standards. Those unable to pay rushed into the market and drove up house prices to unaffordable levels. Each demon had its own role to play in the double-demon meltdown event of 2008. To sum up, the lack of credit standards much amplified the risk of leveraged speculation. Leveraged speculation vastly amplified the risk of lax credit standards. But each side vested its own inner demon with angelic qualities.

More broadly speaking, neither liberals nor conservatives ever got it right about how evolution shaped human behavior. Both philosophies do contain some valid insights. Conservatives clearly see the need for individuals to have civil rights that include economic freedom to innovate, to get ahead. Liberals, of course, recognize the need for human communities to care for each other in hard times. But conservatives drag a very big anchor by buying into the "economic man" model of human behavior as a major foundation of classical and then neoclassical Keynesian economics, albeit with liberal help, as we shall shortly see. This caricature called economic man was not only completely self-centered, he was also entirely rational in all his decisions, whether consuming or investing—a veritable Mr. Spock. What is more, Mr. Spock always had complete market information. If such creatures have emerged anywhere in the cosmos it was probably somewhere within another galaxy on a planet, perhaps called Vulcan, where evolution produced purely rational creatures such as Mr. Spock.

Now there are two justifications for keeping this Mr. Spock in the neoclassical model. The first we owe to Milton Friedman. He held that no one pretends economic man is a real portrait of human behavior. Instead it is simply an instrument, Friedman insisted, a mere abstraction from reality that allows us to make better predictions purely within the domain of economic competition. That is perhaps true for about 20 percent of our behavior in the economic domain. In the other 80 percent, economic man gives us scads of false predictions that are often 180 degrees off, and often with ghastly outcomes. For example, the whole phenomenon of communism could not have evolved in a population of pure individualists concerned only with themselves. Nor could workers have formed trade unions. But if somehow they had done so, their pure rationality would prevent them from intentionally suffering economic loss by going out on strike knowing they could not win any advantage, but striking nonetheless to show union solidarity.

The second justification is that economists deliberately set up this unreal caricature for the same reason that physicists might suppose a pure vacuum when calculating the baseline speed of an airplane. They of course know that airplanes do not fly in a vacuum, and that they must at a later stage, add air and the aerodynamic drag (a form of friction) that it produces into their calculations. Since the amount of drag will vary depending on the qualities of the air (density, temperature, velocity, etc.), it makes sense to add variables later, once the baseline is established. The trouble with this analogy is that economists make their baseline calculations with their economic man and then usually fail to add the particular variables of any real-world situation. They do not add in factors for bonds of loyalty, esprit de corps or its absence, morale, cultural or other values that might trump economic motivation, and so on. Thus, by default economic man's rationality still dominates, but in these days, liberals keep Mr. Spock out of sight in the back office.

John Maynard Keynes famously refuted the claim that purely rational calculation governed economic decisions. He coined the phrase "animal spirits" to describe what drives many human decisions and most especially including economic decisions. Keynes recognized that "animal spirits" accounted for the Wall Street Crash of 1929 and most earlier crashes going back to the Dutch tulip bulb mania of 1636–37. But it is also true that ever since Keynes made that point in his 1936 masterwork, *The General Theory of Employment Interest and Money*, his followers have marginalized those "animal spirits" to the point of near extinction in favor of a gradually renewed primacy of the rational economic man, though again, they keep the purely rational Mr. Spock out of sight in the back office.

Robert Shiller and George Akerlof, in their book,[2] put it this way:

> [After the publication of Keynes's book] . . . Keynes's followers rooted out almost all of the animal spirits—the non-economic motives and irrational behaviors—that lay at the heart of his explanations of the Great Depression. They left just enough animal spirits to yield a Least-Common Denominator theory that minimized the intellectual distance between *The General Theory* . . . and the standard classical economics of the day. In the standard theory [of economic man] there are no animal spirits. People act only for economic motives and they only act rationally. . . . [and a few lines later] This new classical view . . . was passed from economists to

think-tankers, policy elites, and public intellectuals, and finally to the mass media. It became a political mantra, "I am a believer in the free markets." . . . No limits were set on the excesses of Wall Street. It got wildly drunk and now the world must face the consequences.

This post-1980 enthusiastic faith in the power of free markets is associated mainly with President Reagan and Britain's Margaret Thatcher in the mass media. But note that Shiller and Akerlof are clear that this marginalization of Keynes's "animal spirits" was carried out by Keynes's (overwhelming) liberal followers. The two authors apologetically explain it by saying that liberals wanted to minimize the distance between themselves and the conservatives to gain acceptance for Keynes's other views.

Personally, I doubt that. I myself was a graduate student in business and economics at the then liberal University of Washington in Seattle just when the new Keynesian thought had taken over. Being a proud conservative, I was well aware of how liberals joyfully criticized conservatives at the time, over 20 years after Keynes wrote his book.

I suspect the reason liberals resurrected the rational Mr. Spock, was much more practical and technological. The rational economic man was newly resurrected because the innovation and success of the mainframe computer gave them a major incentive to resurrect him. Up to about 1960, my liberal professors at the University of Washington were delighted to trash the conservative philosophy. They called it anachronistic, reactionary, or retro. We conservatives were Neanderthals, rooted in the eighteenth century. Liberals showed plenty of animal spirit delight in bragging how much more modern and up-to-date Keynesian theory was for the twentieth century and its maturing industrial revolution.

When mainframe computers reached academia (beginning about 1960) a rather sudden shift began. Quantitative methods began taking over business schools and economics because mainframe computers, crude even as they were, allowed economists to make the necessary mathematical calculations without hiring battalions of mathematicians. The mainframe seemed to allow economics, which was the first academic discipline to call itself a science, to become a real science at long last. By 1960 liberal economists began to tell themselves: We can now make accurate predictions, which, after all, is what a real science does. It was on this issue that the conservative and liberal economists began seeing common ground. But for liberals to join in and participate in this restored science, they had to accept the free market. Many liberals began quietly to distance themselves from Marxist scripture. The Cold War helped. Moreover, both communism and fascism were all for animal spirits. Neither one made a place for the rational Mr. Spock. Each one aimed to restore a sense of community, one they claimed capitalism's industrial revolution had destroyed. Both volubly called upon animal spirits to energize the masses to a new revolutionary fervor. Mr. Spock was not wanted.

The difference between them was simply that Marxists wanted to do away with the nation state and ethnic and tribal loyalty in favor of worldwide working class solidarity. For their part the Fascists wanted to marshal ethnic and tribal loyalty precisely to focus it on the nation state. The battle between them came down to whether they would marshal animal spirits in the cause of international socialism or on behalf of National Socialism. (In Germany, this term eventually yielded the truncation Nazi. Although Hitler demonstrated that Fascism lent itself to virulent racism, Mussolini and Franco proved that it was not inherent in it. Neither of these thirties-era fascist leaders from Italy and Spain promoted racism.)

Meanwhile, back at the academic ranch, the new mainframe computer's emergence in the sixties had changed everything. To let Keynes's animal spirits run loose would kill economics as a mechanistic science after the model of Isaac Newton's mechanistic physics. Newton envisaged a mechanistic and mathematically linear universe. So, many liberal and even conservative neoclassical economists quickly embraced a mechanistic market universe devoid of animal spirits. Those spirits would quash their claim that economics was a real science. Economists of all persuasions were guilty of "physics envy." Neoclassical economists needed a mechanistic universe to make accurate forecasts based on the linear mathematics that mainframes handle so well. Animal spirits simply had to be airbrushed out that newly rational world.

As mainframe mania took over (more animal spirits on the loose) the criteria for "publish or perish" took on a whole new character for professors seeking tenure and promotion. In the top tier universities, economics professors not only had to publish, they had to publish articles in scholarly journals that demonstrated their command of quantitative methods such as linear programming. The idea that economics was now a real science took on new and vibrant urgency. That idea also began taking over business management, thanks to one of its most famous promoters, namely Robert McNamara, President Kennedy's Secretary of Defense. He coined the term "management science" to distinguish it from the failed concept of "scientific management," and he was justified by the computer's new ability to make "accurate forecasts" of the economy.[3]

So, you did not like calculus? Forget about becoming a tenured professor or being promoted in the big research universities after the mainframes took over.

Here, now, we come to the point. Suddenly the utility of Mr. Spock, our wholly rational economic man, was clear. Science is presumably the soul of reason and so there is no room here for animal spirits. Machines do not have animal spirits, and thus the mechanistic Mr. Spock was born again. But his resurrection from the grave Keynes had put him in was, again let us be clear, discreet. Liberals did not promote Mr. Spock, they just quit criticizing the rational economic man. They simply ignored what Keynes had said about animal spirits. Liberal textbooks such as the one pioneered by Paul Samuelson of MIT ignored all that. But Mr. Spock remained alive and well, in what was now called the *Neoclassical Model*.

Again, the reason is clear. If economic man was left to rest in peace in his grave, and twentieth century economics was turned over to animal spirits, then economists' newly computerized ability to make accurate predictions would have looked as silly as in fact it proved to be, even before 2008. The claim to accurate predictions required economists to assume people do behave rationally more or less all the time. The problem is that people in the real world often do not behave rationally. But, if they posit rational humans, professors can then go on and formulate equations that have precise answers. They can give their students tests that require them to calculate such precise answers (within the domain of rational human behavior). Again, let Keynes's animal spirits loose in the real world of economics, and the stampede would quash the project of upgrading economics to a real (mechanistic) science on a par with (mechanistic) physics.

The Faustian bargain between liberals and conservatives that helped bring about the subprime mortgage collapse was in that context mainly political. But in many ways it grew out of a similar bargain struck in academia in the sixties that allowed both liberals and conservatives to use Mr. Spock, each for their own purposes. But as a witness to Mr. Spock's resurrection as a liberal, let me assure the reader that without real world animal spirits on the part of liberal professors, that resurrection could not have occurred. They were absolutely passionate in hammering the skeptics of quantification and its claim to be scientific. Liberal economists who did not convert to this new quantified and thus "scientific" world were given short shrift.

Perhaps the most noted of those who crossed the finish line before the mainframe took hold was the highly popular John Kenneth Galbraith. His book sales far exceeded those of any other economist, right, left, or center. Behind the scenes, however, Galbraith was widely panned by many of his liberal colleagues because he used history, not quantitative methods, as a guide. Galbraith survived because he became a big name in economics before the mainframe computer had taken over in academia. Besides, he could laugh all the way to the bank, thanks to the series of best sellers he had written. Galbraith already had tenure, a full professorship, and scads of Harvard students who wanted to take his class. But it was Galbraith's huge popular following that made him most contemptible to quant liberals, animated by that animal spirit we call envy. The quant guys knew their computer printouts would never grab an audience the way Galbraith's clever writing did. The irony is that Galbraith, more than any other liberal, made Keynes's theories—with animal spirits mostly airbrushed out—well known and accepted by many business executives and other people who never took economics.

I often disagreed with Galbraith, but I read everything he wrote because he wrote so well. His historical approach was always enlightening. He could be at one and the same time amusing, interesting, and informative. That was true even when Galbraith was dead wrong. (His theory that corporate America could and did manipulate consumers via mass advertising to assure their own profits collapsed in the early seventies.) Madison Avenue's copywriters could not and did not prevent the stagflation—simultaneous high unemployment and high inflation—from 1973 to 1983.) In all his writings, however, Galbraith was openly contemptuous of the idea that economic man was a rational Mr. Spock-like creature devoid of greed. In fact, toward the end of his life, Galbraith joined forces with a worldwide revolt against neoclassical economics. The revolt began in France under the unfortunate name of Post-Autistic Economics. (The French apply the term "autistic" more broadly than do Americans.) A loud chorus is arising that neoclassical economics has created an abstract quantified world that hardly relates to the messy actual world driven by animal spirits in which we live. Students everywhere are now beginning to object. The academicians from the great research universities such as Harvard, Yale, Chicago, UCLA, MIT, and Princeton so far refuse to give up their great faith in the mechanistic quantitative approach. Why? Because they have a huge intellectual investment in the neoclassical model that depends on a Mr. Spock-like economic man. Myron Scholes, who was interviewed after the crash of his Long Term Credit Management Hedge Fund, put his finger on the problem: "We knew our math," Scholes said, but "we ignored our history." Scholes might have added that history was and still is driven by the animal spirits that the quantitative guys had airbrushed out of Keynes.

In the context of 2008, political liberals are vocal about how wrong conservatives were to promote *laissez-faire* together with leveraged speculation. Liberals just ignore the fact that liberal academic economists, such as Myron Scholes, justified deregulation by claiming that quantitative methods removed the risk of leverage while making no allowance for greed. Once, thanks to both liberals and conservatives, deregulation abolished those post-Depression constraints designed to limit the free expression of our animal spirits, it was just such free expression—in the form of greed when speculating—that gave us 2008.

NOTES

1. *The Gods That Failed*, p. 247.
2. Shiller, Robert, and George Akerlof. *Animal Spirits: How Human Psychology Drives the Economy, and Why It Matters for Global Capitalism.* Princeton, NJ: Princeton University Press, 2009.
3. I examined Mr. McNamara's philosophy in my book *Postmodern Management,* in the chapter entitled "Forecasting, Planning, Command, and Control."

Chapter 7

THE FINAL COLLAPSE IN OCTOBER 2008

Cold War communists often spoke of the "correlation of forces" that led to this or that result. Most outcomes, in short, result from a complicated complex or combination of other outcomes and those with others yet, and so on. So it is with the collapse of 2008. That outcome also resulted from a complex combination of other events. In the last chapter we saw how liberals and conservatives both helped bring about the subprime mortgage bubble and did so in such a way that guaranteed the bubble would burst. Yet that bargain could only have been struck because of a chain of inter-related events that set the stage for it.

First, the financial sector had to be deregulated. But that would not likely have happened except for the emergence of Keynesian theory in 1936 and mainframe computers in 1952. This convergence subsequently led to the return of *homo economicus*. The new computers had made it practical for economists to solve complex mathematical algorithms and appear to be scientific. One of those newly practical algorithms suggested that the risk could largely be taken out of leveraged speculation. Even so, to take that as a serious proposition, it was necessary to assume that investors were always rational, Spock-like creatures. Yet Keynes's newly prevailing economic theory spoke of the animal spirits of speculators—including their greed—as a cause of Wall Street's collapse of 1929. In other words, Keynes recognized that investors were not rational Mr. Spock-like creatures, and that leverage could turn investors trying to get rich quick into greedy pigs. So for that reason, Keynes's liberal followers had to airbrush the animal spirits out of his theory. This was done discreetly. They just ignored what Keynes said about animal spirits. They also quit attacking economic man (Mr. Spock) and accommodated him as a mere instrumental device. But they did not do so until the mainframe had begun to prove itself. Out of all this emerged what we now call the Neoclassical Model.

Keeping Mr. Spock also solved another problem. Keynesian economics did not pretend to address growth. Keynes, after all, was mainly concerned with what had to be done to recover from the Great Depression since the free market had apparently failed to do so. However, America's economy had grown steadily over the postwar period, and by 1973, the prosperity was heady. Both political parties made growth a prime economic goal. It was also clear that capitalism had proven a far more dynamic engine of growth than socialism. By the seventies, strong arguments were being made that leveraged speculation could foster the economic growth by creating new wealth, and using our computers, we could devise methods to spread the risk so that no speculative bubbles would burst.

All this was exciting stuff. Suddenly, finance was seen as the key sector destined to be the new engine of growth. Bankers, brokers, and financial economists all innovated a whole suite of new ways to practice leveraged speculation. The favorite innovations involved new financial debt instruments such as derivatives, collateralized debt obligations (CDOs), securitized mortgages, credit default swaps, and others. But those new instruments all involved converting savings into debt, and the American culture, influenced by its Puritan work ethic, had made savings a prime economic and quasi-spiritual virtue. In addition, Keynes's animal spirits posed a threat to legitimizing leveraged speculation after the crash of 1929. Once the animal spirits were airbrushed out of Keynes's theory, however, it could be employed to buttress the cause of speculation because it clearly discounted savings as an economic virtue. Indeed, Keynes made savings suspect by identifying it as part of the cause of the Great Depression. And having discounted savings, Keynes elevated spending as the new economic virtue, the source of recovery from depression. Spending, in fact, was good even when it required going into debt to do so. That anti-savings aspect of Keynes's theory helped make leveraged speculation a good thing—in the hands of Mr. Spock of course. As Keynes himself might have put it, such was the thinking that had been "in the air" for the 30 years prior to the collapse of 2008.

For anyone born after 1960, the use of debt to leverage both our investments and our standard of living seemed as perfectly normal as was cigarette smoking during World War II. Debt became a part of the post–World War II culture. There were always doubters, skeptics, and contrarians, to be sure. Still, many of today's mature adults nearing retirement have lived their lives deep in debt, for cars, mortgages, and credit cards. Young people today have grown up never knowing any other way to live than to leverage their standard of living with debt.

Yet another force, globalization, amplified America's housing bubble as well, and it did so in such a way that when the bubble burst, global financial meltdown quickly resulted. One can argue that globalization began with Magellan and became institutionalized by the British Empire. But the term as used today came into currency after the Cold War ended in 1989, as more powerful microchips evolved to produce much more powerful computers that in turn gave impetus to a newly evolving Internet and World Wide Web. A global correlation of forces now came together. This new combination virtually abolished the time and cost of communication over global distances by enabling ubiquitous mass transfer of digital information. In the financial sector, this development rendered global capital flows largely outside the power of nation states to control. The putative global village had suddenly become very much a reality. And it was not long before the huge, unintended consequence arose.

Thomas L. Friedman has published several books, including *The World Is Flat*, that do a fine job of explaining the positive side of globalization. The flat world he sees and describes, which has arisen from the surge of new electronic technology in the post–Cold War world, offers a much more level competitive playing field to everyone on the planet. The idea that Marxism provided a viable alternative to capitalism collapsed with the fall of the Soviet Union. Russia, China, and India, now relieved of the hobbling constraints of socialism, quickly adapted to competitive capitalism, became much more efficient and competitive, and took their place on the new level playing field of the world market.[1]

In 2005, when *The World Is Flat* came out, Friedman's optimism seemed well placed. David Smick, for example, points out that:

> The last quarter century has been the golden age of poverty reduction, all occurring during the shift toward globalized financial markets. . . . about a billion people have moved out of poverty since 1980. Put another way, during the period 1950 to 1980, when the World Bank and other international agencies were flush with money, there was actually a significant *increase* in global poverty. . . . These well-intentioned efforts suffered because without honest and efficient institutions in recipient countries, the results of government to government transfers will always disappoint.[2]

In his 1968 book, *Asian Drama*, Sweden's Gunnar Myrdal earlier drew a similar conclusion.[3] In fact Myrdal insisted on pointing out the massive corruption of the governments receiving aid from the World Bank, other development banks, the United States Agency for International Development (USAID) and other sources, who, for their part, mostly pretended not to notice. By more or less common consent, they diplomatically airbrushed institutionalized corruption out of the equation, dismissing it as the work of a few "bad apples." They pinned their hope on the Keynesian proposition that capital investment induced an automatic accelerator or multiplier effect on income quite apart from the issue of institutional efficiency. But in fact a great deal, even most of that development capital, was wasted. As an economic consultant overseas for some of that time, I was an eyewitness to much of that waste.

Nevertheless, since 1980, it seemed the computerized Keynesian paradigm had apparently given birth to the greatest growth machine the world had ever seen. It is easy to see why its promoters dismissed skeptics, given the long stretch of seemingly outstanding results. Sure, there had been some bumps in the road, but we had gotten past them all. First, there was the 1982 international banking crisis when Mexico nearly defaulted. But we survived that. Second came the savings and loan crisis and collapse of 1986; that was a big shock but we got over it as well. Then, in 1987, the stock market crashed, in part because of the portfolio insurance debacle that arose from using the strategy of Black and Scholes. We expected a big recession, but none came. Fourth, Kidder Peabody failed in 1994, but who noticed? A fifth bump in the road was the Asian market collapse of 1997. That seemed frightening at first, but recovery quickly followed thanks to globalization. The next year, Myron Scholes's own Long Term Capital Management hedge fund collapsed in the wake of Russia's bond default, and it had to be bailed out. That bump was simply greeted with sniggers about Nobel Prize nerds getting carried away with themselves. The dot-com bubble that began forming in 1998 and collapsed in 2000–2001 was the seventh bump. Still, it mainly seemed to wipe out teenage nerds who had also gotten too carried away with themselves, so why worry? What the heck, one bubble bursts, and another one forms. In the event, the subprime real estate bubble soon began to take up the slack, and by 2004, lots of folks were seeing huge equity growth in house prices and accessing their new-found wealth by taking out big home equity loans. Why let that equity remain idle, for heaven's sake?

The post-1980 Great Globalized Bubble Growth Machine, it seemed, just kept on going. That is until it stopped cold in 2007 and burst in 2008. Bump number eight turned out to be not just one more bump in the road, not even a crash, but a full-blown global disaster.

Yet until the market crashed, it would have taken a great deal of courage for federal officials to intervene. Democracies have a very poor record of doing that sort of thing. The reason is clear: quashing growth amounts to biting the hand that feeds you—that is to say, elects you. During the period when a bubble is forming it truly appears that real wealth is being created and real people are being helped. Few elected officials want to rain on that parade. After all, this "new economy," built more around finance than production, had apparently lifted over a billion people out of poverty worldwide since its 1980 beginning. Even liberals felt constrained from attacking *laissez-faire* too much. The top down government approach had failed over and over again in the postwar years and the Marxist god of communism had collapsed in utter failure by 1991. So we now have a cemetery full of failed gods.

Up to mid 2005, and despite the frequent "bumps," the economy seemed to be doing fine. In 2006 worries began to mount, and by the summer of 2007, it was clear a major crisis was at hand. By early 2008, though, the aggregate statistics seemed to indicate acceptable performance again. But then the wheels came off: the crisis at Bear Stearns; the collapse of Lehman Brothers, then AIG, Freddie Mac, Fannie Mae. The Merrill Lynch takeover by Bank of America; the bank-ruptcy of Washington Mutual and others. . . . In October 2008, the major stock market averages had fallen by about 50 percent from the historic highs posted a year earlier.

All these events have been discussed in great detail in many fine books. For example, Kevin Phillips's book, *Bad Money* (2008), though published before the crash, gives a fine history of the specific policy decisions, such as deregulation, that lead up to it. Phillips includes fascinating historical comparisons of Spain,

Holland, Britain, and America in that order. Phillips shows how each nation rose to power by exploiting a comparative advantage in energy and focused on trade, production, or both. Each then shifted to a focus on finance, that is to say, to making money from returns and interest on investments, which signaled the eclipse of each nation in turn. Phillips then presents strong evidence suggesting that America is headed in the same direction.

Niall Ferguson, in *The Ascent of Money*, lays out the history of the rise and the use of money from the earliest times, but especially since the invention of banking by the Dutch. He takes us through the Dutch tulip bulb bubble, France's Mississippi bubble, and on to Britain's South Sea bubble at about the same time in the eighteenth century. He explains how George Soros and his Quantum Fund, betting against the pound sterling, beat the Bank of England in the early 1990s.[4]

Ferguson displays the Black and Scholes formula for pricing options with the following incisive comment:

> Feeling a bit baffled? Can't follow the algebra? To be honest I am baffled too. But that was just fine with the quants. To make money from this insight, they needed markets full of people who didn't have a clue about how to price options but relied instead on gut instincts.

Ferguson goes on to describe how Myron Scholes and another quant, Harvard Business School's Robert Merton (who made big money using the Black and Scholes model), joined forces with others to create the Long Term Capital Management hedge fund. (The two would later receive the Nobel Prize in Economics; Black, unfortunately, did not live long enough to share in the honor.) Ferguson then explains in detail how LTCM worked and why it collapsed in 1998, a victim of EMH, the efficient market hypothesis. (George Soros, meanwhile, made billions by rejecting EMH.) As Ferguson explains that hypothesis:

> Markets are efficient, meaning that the movement of stock prices cannot be predicted; they are continuous, frictionless and completely liquid; and the returns on stocks follow a normal bell curve distribution.[5]

The market in other words was assumed to be the embodiment of a sort of collective Mr. Spock.

In *The Two Trillion Dollar Meltdown: Easy Money, High Rollers, and the Great Credit Crash* (Public Affairs, 2008), Charles Morris also gives a good account of events leading up to the crash of 2008 and "the great game of risk transfer." As his subtitle suggests, Morris also focuses on the loss of ethics by nearly all participants in those events:

> A common and disheartening threat of the last couple of decades' financial crises, from the Savings and Loan crash through Enron and the credit debacle is the consistent failure of profit making entities as statutory fiduciaries. The securities laws

assume that lawyers, accountants, and credit raters will not allow monetary incentives to override their professional ethics—an assumption that draws little support from the abysmal record.[6]

As are most others, Morris is highly critical of the universal bank. He says baldly, "The universal bank is a bad idea." In his view commercial and investment banks provide different services and should be kept separate. Thus the repeal of Glass-Steagall in 1999 set the stage for creating the bubble that brought us down in 2008.

Larry Elliott and Dan Atkinson, two British journalists, in their book,[7] provide us a British perspective on the financial crisis. In their view, as the subtitle suggests, blind faith in the free markets is what brought us down in the end, and they see the origins of that faith taking shape in the Hotel du Parc on Mount Pelerin overlooking Lake Geneva in 1947 during a meeting of 38 conservatives. The group included such notables as Friedrich von Hayek, Ludwig von Mises, and a youthful Milton Friedman (pp. 48–50). Their goal, according to Elliott and Atkinson, was to "chart the fight-back of classical liberalism against what was seen as the tyranny of the collective." For the rest of the book these folks and their followers are labeled the "New Olympians," a takeoff on the Greek gods who lived on Mount Olympus in ancient Greek mythology. As background, the two give us a historical overview of financial excess dating back to the Dutch tulip bulb mania. They see the New Olympians as opening a Pandora's Box containing six evils: "These are speculation, recklessness, greed, arrogance, oligarchy, and excess." Much of their book is focused on British experience, especially after Margaret Thatcher. They provide interesting accounts of the troubles of British banks such as the failure of Northern Rock. However, the two rather underplay the fact that the god of Marxism had also failed badly by 1991. They do betray a soft spot for British socialism, 1945 to 1960, and of course they did want not to divert attention from the failed god of unconstrained free market speculative excess after the election of President Reagan, and Prime Minister Thatcher.

George Akerlof and Robert J. Shiller, in *Animal Spirits*, point out that Shiller first coined the term "irrational exuberance" in an earlier book. But today the term is also closely associated with Alan Greenspan who used it when describing the dot-com boom. These authors remind us it was John Maynard Keynes, back in 1936, who first suggested that animal spirits, rather than Spock-like rationality, accounted for the irrational exuberance that accompanies leveraged speculation. The authors also give their view of why liberals felt they had to airbrush Keynes's psychology of animal spirits—that is of real human beings—out of Keynes's macroeconomics. They claim it was to avoid undue controversy with conservatives. I would not dispute that such a motive played a part, but I think it overlooks much. In particular, it ignores the fact that this shift did not come until the arrival of the mainframe computer; suddenly it seemed that Keynesian economics could aspire to be a real science, if it also had the services of *homo economicus*.

Only then did we hear about the neoclassical model instead of just Keynesian macroeconomics.[8]

Panic: The Story of Modern Financial Insanity (Norton, 2009), edited by Michael Lewis, is mainly a collection of previously written articles that occasionally provide insights into events leading up to 2008. The best of these articles, by Michael Lewis himself, gives an insider's account of the stock market crash of October 19, 1987. He is particularly clear about how the Black and Scholes type of risk avoidance strategy backfired, indeed failed so badly that it actually brought down the market.[9]

George Soros[10] provides a fascinating personal account of his own success as a financial speculator by rejecting Mr. Spock. Much as I did from a much different perspective, Soros saw through the notion that markets were always rational. He did so while attending the London School of Economics. (Soros emigrated to England in 1947 from communist Hungary.) From that insight Soros has promoted an alternative view, which he calls "reflexivity." His main point is that a feedback loop can arise between markets and investors, that they interact, that the actions of one can and do feedback to influence the actions of the other. Long frustrated by the fact that economists ignored his theory, he began to describe himself as a failed philosopher, even though he put his philosophy to work with great success, making billions as a speculator. But, Soros insists, if the conventional view of a rational market was correct, and markets did move in a random walk toward some equilibrium point, then it would have been impossible for him to have been as successful as he was over so long a period of time.

Soros finally concluded that his reflexivity theory failed to convince others because it did not lend itself to quantitative forecasting. In a word, all the quants hated it. They cared only for Mr. Spock's rationality, which gave great scope for those Black and Scholes kind of equations and clear predictions. But failed philosopher though he was, Soros could laugh all the way to the bank.

William D. Cohan is a journalist who chronicled the collapse of Bear Stearns in his book *House of Cards: A Tale of Hubris and Wretched Excess on Wall Street* (Doubleday, 2009). He provides an almost hour by hour account of the company's final week in March of 2008 and documents how the company's heavy purchase of subprime mortgage bundles, once they became "toxic assets," contributed to Bear Stearns's demise.[11]

Another insider account, *A Colossal Failure of Common Sense: The Inside Story of the Collapse of Lehman Brothers*, comes from former Lehman Brothers vice president Lawrence G. McDonald.[12] He begins his story of getting to the "big time" with an account of his career in which he struggled tirelessly to get there. He relates his utter dismay with what happened after he joined Lehman Brothers. Whereas Bear Stearns was saved by the intervention of the Fed, Lehman was allowed to collapse, go bankrupt, and cease to exist. McDonald reveals a good bit of personal bitterness about what happened, and especially about the role played by Lehman CEO Richard Fuld. According to McDonald, Fuld ignored warning after warning about the wild risks he was taking with subprime mortgages. But Fuld bulled ahead anyway, ultimately bringing Lehman down. McDonald thus made "the failure of common sense" a key part of his book's title.

Economist Thomas Sowell, in *The Housing Boom and Bust* already quoted earlier, zeros in on the subprime mortgage fiasco. He recounts the role played by the Community Reinvestment Act of 1977 that empowered organizations such as ACORN (Association of Community Organizations for Reform Now) to harass banks into making subprime loans. Sowell also relates the sad story of how Fannie Mae and Freddie Mac enabled banks making subprime mortgages to lay off the risk on Fannie and Freddie, who promptly passed that risk on to other investors who thought they were investing in relatively risk-free bundles with a AAA credit rating. This story has been told many times, but Sowell also documents the role that environmental protection laws and codes played in pushing up housing prices. He shows that in communities with tough restrictions such as on the West Coast, Washington DC, Florida, and parts of New York, among others, prices rose far higher than in other communities.

The above analyses all have valid insights. There is much agreement on the role played by financial deregulation. It licensed highly leveraged speculation that led to rampant greed, predatory lending, and obscene bonuses and other payments to top management, especially in finance. All this, many agree, was much amplified by the repeal of the Glass-Steagall banking act that kept commercial banks and investment banks separate. A few mentioned how such license spread to the other professions such as law, accounting, and credit rating agencies. More than a few people in these professions simply sold out in order to cut themselves in on the swag rather than doing their job of blowing the whistle. The temptations were just too great to ignore. In short, these authors implicitly agree about the moral hazard that arose by licensing highly leveraged speculation, that came to engulf nearly the whole economy, and that played a major role in bringing down that economy.

All these authors are clear that blind faith in the free market accounted for much of this lapse. The true believers thus refused to acknowledge clear signs of danger. That was true for most of the Bush Administration. This group of officials includes Alan Greenspan and Ben Bernanke of the Federal Reserve Board, Henry Paulson at Treasury, Chris Cox, head of the Security and Exchange Commission, along with nearly all the key officials in the investment banks, such as Merrill Lynch, Bear Stearns, Lehman Brothers, Goldman Sachs, and the rest. The same was true for many commercial banks as well, most notably in Citibank, Washington Mutual, and Wachovia, and for large mortgage lenders such as Countrywide. And it was also true for most of the hedge funds and private equity funds.

But liberals had their own role to play, most particularly in setting up the housing industry for the subprime mortgage bubble that triggered the global financial collapse when it finally burst. Liberal Congressmen such as Barney Frank, who headed the House Finance Committee, and Senator Chris Dodd, who headed the same committee in the Senate, enthusiastically supported the subprime mortgage market with its NINJA loans. The widespread distribution of those toxic derivative assets throughout the global financial market was the specific cause of the global financial crash. In their compassion to make affordable housing accessible to minorities and the poor, and by encouraging and even demanding NINJA loans be extended to further their "compassionate" goal, they were blind to simple common sense.

But only two of the above authors, Soros and Shiller, touch on the overriding issue that made all the rest possible. I refer to the insistence by both liberal and conservative economists that the field of economics could provide reliably accurate forecasts based on truly scientific, quantitative methods. They refuse to admit that in principle they cannot make reliably accurate forecasts in the image of Isaac Newton's astronomy. For both liberals and conservatives this "physics envy" motivated the retention of *homo economicus*. The Keynesian liberals and *laissez-faire* conservatives put different spins on it, but both supported *homo economicus* long after the Great Depression had proved that myth to be balderdash. The cautionary lesson here is this: A strongly held ideology seems able to bulletproof "true believers" against all evidence that their ideology is deeply flawed.

A final point in this review is that none of the above authors ever seems to realize that the greed licensed by financial deregulation did great damage even to nonfinancial companies by disrupting the post-1980 quality and customer service reforms driven by Japanese competition. Huge bonuses seduced otherwise good managers away from continuing to pursue the organic reforms that fostered cooperative teamwork and self-motivated, grassroots efficiency. Company officers and directors discovered, when the prospect of huge bonuses appeared, that the adversarial relationship between management and labor served their purposes just fine. As explained earlier, they could again treat employees as so many undifferentiated units of labor, and as such commodities, they could be cast aside with impunity by acts likely to lead to huge bonuses.

In Part II of this book we will turn to these broader issues of ideology. We will see why Charles Darwin's flawed assumption of "uniformitarianism" diverted economists from seeing the evolution of economies as a part of the broader field of evolution. That diversion played a big role in economists' preference for abstract models. Those models led model builders largely to ignore historical trends, including clear patterns of boom and bust. When detached from history, those models often fail badly, as Myron Scholes discovered when his Long Term Capital Management Fund crashed. No thanks to Darwin, we will look at the overwhelming historical evidence that cultural economies evolve in a process similar to biology but with a difference. We will see that human innovations in technology do drive cultural evolution, much as mutations in DNA drive the evolution of anatomy. Otherwise, cultures and anatomy both evolve by a process that incorporates boom and bust.

NOTES

1. Friedman, Thomas L. *The Earth Is Flat: A Brief History of the 21st Century.* New York: Picador, 2007. See also *The Lexus and the Olive Tree*, 1999.

2. Smick, David. *The World Is Curved: Hidden Dangers of the Global Economy.* New York: Penguin Press, 2008, p. 321.

3. Myrdal, Gunnar. *Asian Drama.* New York: Penguin, 1968.

4. Ferguson, Niall. *The Ascent of Money: A Financial History of the World.* New York: Penguin Press, 2008, p. 321.

5. Ibid., pp. 321–325.

6. Morris, Charles. *The Two Trillion Dollar Meltdown: Easy Money, High Rollers, and the Great Credit Crash.* New York: Public Affairs Books, 2009, p. 150.

7. Elliott, Larry, and Dan Atkinson. *The Gods That Failed: How Blind Faith in Markets Has Cost Us Our Future.* New York: Nation Books, 2009.

8. Akerlof, George, and Robert Shiller. *Animal Spirits: How Human Psychology Drives the Economy and Why It Matters for Global Capitalism.* Princeton University Press, 2009.

9. Lewis, Michael, editor. *Panic: The Story of Modern Financial Insanity.* New York: Norton, 2009. Introduction, and page 36.

10. Soros, George. *The Crash of 2008: The New Paradigm for Financial Management.* New York: Public Affairs, 2008.

11. Cohan, William C. *House of Cards: A Tale of Hubris and Wretched Excess on Wall Street.* New York: Doubleday, 2009.

12. McDonald, Lawrence C. *A Colossal Failure of Common Sense: The Inside Story of the Collapse of Lehman Brothers.* New York: Crown Publishers, 2009.

Part II

DARWIN'S GAP

Chapter 8

UNIFORMITARIANISM

C harles Darwin was truly one of the great minds of the modern world. He helped transform the nineteenth century and his influence remains strong to this day. His theory of evolution held that if random mutations in our genes improved an individual's fitness, that mutation would naturally tend to survive, reproduce, and establish itself in succeeding generations. A major breakthrough in understanding life, Darwin's theory has had to withstand bitter and prolonged objections from some religious quarters because it departs from the Genesis account. That account cannot be either modified or supplanted, these people assert, because it is the divinely revealed Truth of God. Darwin's theory, in effect substituting randomness for God's divine direction of life's evolution, in this view can only be seen as blasphemy.

Quite apart from the religious objection, though, Darwin's theory was incomplete. Moreover, it contained a major flaw. The flaw was Darwin's belief in physical uniformitarianism, a belief that long inhibited economic theory from embracing economic history. (It was not until comparatively recently that geologists finally gave up on uniformitarianism.) Economic history offers a very clear example of evolution in action at the level of culture. Culture does indeed evolve, and in much the same way as biology. Yet Darwin never acknowledged as much, and in that sense, his theory of evolution was also incomplete.

I addressed this issue in my previous book.[1] It embraces the Gould-Eldredge thesis that evolution does not evolve in the smooth and continuous way Darwin thought. Rather, things evolve by fits and starts, sudden jumps followed by often longer periods of stability.

That thesis, called *punctuated equilibrium*, has now become mainstream. The process of fits and starts is precisely the way human economies and cultures evolve. But no major theory of economics embraces that fact, including the currently prevailing neoclassical theory. Darwin adopted uniformitarianism from Charles Lyell, the founder of modern geology as a science. Lyell correctly saw the evidence that the earth was hundreds of millions of years old, far older than the approximate 6,000 years according to the biblical account. Lyell decided that the course of geologic evolution was slow and gradual, and shaped by the same processes that we witness today. He insisted geology was not driven by major catastrophes. Lyell had no real proof for his assumption. Lyell simply proclaimed uniformitarianism. He rejected catastrophic explanations because, many suspect, those explanations lent credence to the biblical account contained in Genesis. At the time, science in general was breaking free of the efforts of some clergy to use "divinely revealed Truth" to veto scientific explanations at odds with those of Christian tradition.

Darwin felt this same need, to separate his account of evolution from the biblical stories and declare independence from Genesis. Knowing his account would raise a storm, he sat on his findings for nearly 20 years. Only in 1859, upon learning that Alfred Russell Wallace had developed his own theory of evolution with similar conclusions and was planning to publish them, did Darwin, intent to be first, rush his own book into print.

Since Darwin, we have come to assume that science has broken free of being subject to religious veto. But now, a new effort appears underway to bring back such a veto, an effort driven by Islam. On November 20, 2009 the Associated Press reported that various Muslim groups are preparing to petition the United Nations to impose sanctions on anyone who blasphemes sacred religious dogma. The article said, "Documents obtained by the Associated Press show that Algeria and Pakistan have taken the lead in lobbying to eventually bring the proposal to a vote in the General Assembly."[2] In essence, the proposal would prevent saying anything to offend religious belief. (See Appendix E for an examination of the influence of Islam on our economy.)

Darwin's desire to declare independence from Genesis is understandable. Still, his uniformitarianism proved to be false. Catastrophes have indeed driven much of the earth's geological evolution. Asteroid hits, massive volcanoes–in series, huge methane eruptions, earthquakes, floods and tidal waves along with plate tectonics account for much of our geology, and for that matter, our biology. We now know of about six major near-extinction events each of which killed off up to 90 percent of all species. Neither Lyell nor Darwin, of course, had seen the evidence of this. All the same, catastrophes such as earthquakes, floods, and volcanoes clearly played a big and well-documented part of recorded history. Yet, only in the last half of the twentieth century did geologists accept as valid the evidence of these geological catastrophes. Uniformitarianism was still being taught to me by college biology professors in the 1950s. Today, however, science has discarded uniformitarianism as a disproven paradigm and allowed for the fact of catastrophic change.

By the time uniformitarianism was at last banished from mainstream science, neoclassical economics was embedded as the standard academic understanding of economics. Most "academic fortresses" resist change from outside the discipline. But the neoclassical theory of economics also had Wall Street on its side. Wall Street liked the neoclassical theory because it embraced the profit-maximizing

Mr. Spock. It also obligingly dehumanized workers to impersonal commodities, giving rise to the commodity theory of labor. Commodities can be discarded and thus the theory gave an ideal cover for Wall Street's anti-social greed.

It took about 25 years for Gould and Eldredge to see their thesis of punctuated equilibrium widely accepted, shortly before Gould died in 2002. Uniformitarianism's demise, of course, clearly made the idea of sharp punctuations of evolutionary change more acceptable. If geological evolution was punctuated by asteroid hits, massive volcanoes, earthquakes, floods or tsunamis, why was not biology? And for that matter, why not cultures and their economies? That was the question I asked myself when I began to write *Techno-Cultural Evolution*. I asked that question because economic history easily fit the pattern of punctuated equilibrium. Moreover, major cycles of economic growth clearly had been driven by a series of innovations in new technology, especially from the fifteenth century on. For several thousand years before that time there were few innovations and little or no growth in per capita incomes.

Differences in living standards between cultures depended on geography, climate, and available natural resources. According to economic historians nearly all the innovations necessary to permit the rise of civilization and to sustain it had been made before civilization arose. Yet wherever civilizations in the ancient world took hold, internal innovations nearly shut down. Again, that historical record suggested punctuated equilibrium on a long time scale. My work as a research economist at Boeing in the early sixties, meanwhile, suggested the growth of individual innovations followed a pattern that seemed coherent with punctuated equilibrium on a shorter time scale.

Thomas Kuhn's 1962 work[3] also concluded that the history of science was marked by a pattern of sudden jumps, or paradigm shifts, followed by much longer periods of relative stability that Kuhn called "normal science." Indeed Kuhn had begun his work assuming, much like Darwin, that science progressed along a smooth and continuous path over time. Each generation of scientists, he thought, added their bit to the total picture. By the time he finished his research, however, Kuhn concluded the actual history of science did not support that assumption of continuous progress. There were too many sudden jumps, and they marked major changes in the course of scientific inquiry.

Kuhn pointed out, for example, that the Ptolemaic paradigm in astronomy, which had the earth as the center of the universe and the sun and the planets revolving around it, lasted for about 1,500 years. Then, that earth-centered view was suddenly called into question by the Polish priest Nicolaus Copernicus (1473–1543), early in the sixteenth century. He said that many anomalies in the Ptolemaic system could be resolved if one assumed the sun was the fixed center around which the earth and all the other planets orbited. But it took Galileo's observations with his self-made telescope (an invention by a Dutch spectacle craftsman) to confirm that what Copernicus proposed was indeed correct.

And then it took Johannes Kepler and Isaac Newton to work out the math and the physics. Kepler showed how the planets, in elliptical orbits, swept out equal distances of space in equal times despite variances in orbital velocity. Then Newton went on to discover the inverse square law of gravity (that attraction increases or decreases by the square of the distance between bodies) and the three laws of motion (force = mass × acceleration; the law of inertia, that bodies in motion stay in motion until stopped, and they remain stopped until a force moves them; and three, that for every action there is an opposite and equal reaction). Finally, Newton, using his newly invented calculus, was able to solve the equations involving motion satisfactorily. With Newton's discoveries, the Ptolemaic paradigm collapsed. The Copernican/Newtonian paradigm took over, and with that event classical modern physics was born in the seventeenth century.

Kuhn pointed to subsequent shifts from one paradigm to another, such as Einstein's theory of relativity that so profoundly marked the limits of Newtonian physics, and the even more startling wave/particle duality of all matter that is the core of quantum physics.

Wherever I looked in history, in other words, I saw evidence of the kind of pattern that Gould-Eldredge called punctuated equilibrium. Nowhere did I see any long-term pattern that conformed to Darwin's uniformitarianism. Periods of equilibrium, of course, imply relatively uniform conditions for a time. Yet, over the long haul, uniformity always seems to get punctuated by sudden change. Not until 2002 did I see how and why uniformitarianism had inhibited the development of economic theory by virtually foreclosing most of the lessons of history, not just in economics, but in other social sciences as well. Few of them consult the lessons of evolution when devising theories that explain how and why their disciplines have changed over time. Jared Diamond, for example, has given us a coherent account of why human society evolved from its egalitarian origins through a series of shifts to a system marked by sharply defined hierarchy. In a process of increasing social authority, some men were first appointed head-men, then there were weak chiefs, going on to strong chiefs, followed by chiefdoms, then kings and finally god-kings in the ancient world. That succession was clearly a case of evolution in action. (See Chapter 14 of his *Guns, Germs, and Steel*.)[4]

As a result of the gap between economic theory and the real world it sought to describe, the theory descended into a world of abstraction, a development that played a key role in the collapse of 2008. The irony is that a prominent feature of economic history at both the micro and macro level follows a rough pattern of periodic boom and bust. That pattern repeats itself over and over again, in the course of economic history just as it does in political history and biological evolution. Economies, nations, empires, cultures, and civilizations all rise and fall, often to become extinct. The key feature of the punctuated moments of punctuated equilibrium is a process of boom and bust, and to that feature we turn next in Chapter 9.

NOTES

1. Wallace, William McDonald. *Techno-Cultural Evolution: Cycles of Creation and Conflict*. Dulles, VA: Potomac Books, 2006.

2. Associated Press. Nov. 20, 2004.

3. Kuhn, Thomas. *The Structure of Scientific Revolutions*. Chicago: University of Chicago Press, 1962.

4. Diamond, Jared. *Guns, Germs, and Steel: The Fate of Human Societies*. New York: Norton, 1999.

Chapter 9

PUNCTUATED EQUILIBRIUM AND THE FROCA PROCESS

Steven J. Gould and Niles Eldredge finally corrected Darwin's theory by ridding it of uniformitarianism. That correction meant that Darwin's theory could also be integrated into economics and perhaps the other social sciences such as political science and anthropology. Darwin, in effect, kept evolution in a semi-equilibrium state of smooth and very gradual change that was quite unrealistic and fit few facts in any of the social sciences. What Gould and Eldredge added was the "punctuation" where most of the change takes place.[1]

My own 2006 book[2] sought to unpack the punctuation segment and came up with a five-step process that I called FROCA, an acronym that stands for Frontier, Release, Overexploited Opportunity, Crash, and finally Adaptation. Those are in fact the steps that mark the progress of nearly any kind of boom to bust event. It is also the process that restores equilibrium after a major disruption upsets a stable ecosystem.

It works as follows. A disruption of some kind occurs that is serious enough to upset a stable ecosystem. Life is, of course, a competitive struggle for survival, and fitness to survive is calibrated to the existing ecosystem. In fact, the existing ecosystem became stable because a balance of power was achieved among the species making up that ecosystem. That balance is why competition no longer brings about change. No one species can make much progress against any other. It compares to an economy run by a series of private cartels. Predators may still bring down prey, but mainly these are the weaker individuals, and thus the overall strength of the group is maintained so that it is able to survive, with always only its weakest members getting culled out. A competitive balance has evolved, so to speak, a balance, in turn, that evolved out of the punctuated FROCA process.

When, however, a major disruption does occur, that balance of power is badly upset, and sometimes very quickly. Once it is irremediably upset, a new and often chaotic frontier emerges—the initial, F stage of the FROCA process. Some species, perfectly fit within the old equilibrium, may find themselves unfit to survive in the new circumstances, and they will perish. That fact results in what many ecologists call "ecological release" from prior competitive constraints that maintained equilibrium. That is the R part of FROCA. For example, a class of predators may be wiped out or neutralized. Or competitors for the same scarce resources may suffer a similar fate, opening up opportunities for others. That is the O part of FROCA. But it is really a double O, because such opportunities, in the absence of competitive constraints, trigger all-out competition. All-out competition, in turn, almost always tends to exploit the opportunities until exhaustion, that is to say, to overexploit them. When that happens, a crash takes place (the C part of FROCA). When the crash comes, the weakest competitors lose out and many perish. (This is survival-of-the-fittest-in-action.) The strongest survivors must then adapt to the new conditions, now devoid of the frontier's opportunities.) The stage has thus been set for a new equilibrium based on a new balance of power that soon brings all-out competition to an end. That balance also slows or even stops evolutionary change. Competition begets change; a balance of power begets equilibrium. Thus with the final A, adaptation, FROCA has closed the loop. Further evolution awaits a new disruption, another punctuation event that will upset the power balance, change the fitness criteria, and thus trigger another round of FROCA. A new frontier emerges, with new opportunities for a boom, which is followed by another bust leading to a new adaptation to equilibrium. That is the process of evolution, both for biological individuals and for cultures and economies made up of those individuals.

Let us illustrate the FROCA process in the evolution of human biology as well as in human culture and human economies. We will see that, at first, the big changes came in biology, but gradually over the millennia the bigger changes shift to culture. For about the last 300,000 years, more or less, most changes in the way humans live and behave have come in culture. From about 40,000 years ago, nearly all those changes have been cultural. Biologically we are today about what we were 40,000 years ago and even 100,000 years ago. Within those biological parameters, there is wide variation to be sure, but the parameters have not much changed.

Cultural change since then, however, is vast beyond compare. Our cultures evolve so much faster than our anatomy because they have a different driver. It takes mutations, random or otherwise, to change our DNA and thus our anatomy. Those mutations happen to one individual at a time and are passed on only if they provide more fitness. But propagation is much slowed down by the fact that each child contains DNA from both parents so that there is only a 50 percent chance the fit mutation shows up in the newborn child. That is called "sexual dilution." In a very large gene pool, sexual dilution can cause even very fit mutations to die off. Thus, genetic mutations propagate fastest in a small population, perhaps one isolated by a major disruption in the environment.

Sexual dilution does not retard the rate of cultural evolution because new technology drives culture and is the equivalent of mutations. In addition, new technology can work its power of change in whole societies at the same time, not one individual at a time. Moreover, as populations get larger, the new technology can often have a greater impact. Finally, while random change (such as stumbling onto something unexpected) sometimes brings new technology into being, much new technology is deliberate, created to solve specific problems, for example. In a fragmented and competitive world such as ours, that fact makes new technology a self-reinforcing process. Not only is technology a cause of evolution, it is also the result of it. In other words, new technology not only arises out of the FROCA process, but also triggers it. New technology introduced into a stable culture can be disruptive, in part by upsetting the socioeconomic balance of power. In doing those two things it can also change the criteria of fitness in that culture.

Protohumans emerged about 2 million years ago. That first Stone Age culture was characterized by the crudely crafted Oldawan stone tools and weapons associated with *Homo habilis*. As our brains enlarged, our tools got better, with the better-crafted Acheulean tools following soon after. During a series of ice ages, our brain size evolved quickly to that of the 800 cubic centimeters of *Homo erectus*, and by about 300,000 years ago our skulls reached their present size. By then, early humans were making quite sophisticated stone tools and had learned how to use, and later to make, fire. But information about these formative years is too scarce to give a detailed FROCA account without descending deep into speculation. In any event, cultural change up to this point, while gradually getting faster, was still slow and our biology did most of the evolving.

The following quote from Marc Hauser sums up quite well our knowledge of early to late Stone Age human evolution:

> Although anthropologists disagree about exactly when the modern mind took shape, it is clear from the archaeological record that a major transformation occurred during a relative brief period of evolutionary history, starting at approximately 800,000 years ago in the Paleolithic era and crescending about 45,000 to 50,000 years ago. It is during this period of the Paleolithic, an evolutionary eye blink, that we see for the first time multi-part tools, animal bones punctured with holes to fashion musical instruments; burials with accoutrements suggesting beliefs about aesthetics and afterlife; richly symbolic cave paintings that capture in exquisite detail events of the past and the perceived future; and control over fire, a technology that combines our folk physics and psychology and allowed our ancestors to prevail over novel environments by creating warmth and cooking foods to make them edible.[3]

So let us apply FROCA's process of punctuation to the evolution of human culture since the last ice age ended about 12,000 years ago. As Hauser's quote shows, Stone Age technology was well advanced by then. Now with brains of modern size, humans had invented Neolithic technology, and with it they had become the earth's master megafauna predators. That technology had also enabled our ancestors to migrate out of Africa into Eurasia, North and South America, Australia, and in fact everywhere but Antarctica.

Our technology made us such good hunters that we began to overexploit hunting opportunities, local area by local area. But we also became knowledgeable gatherers, and as we overexploited hunting, we were forced to rely ever more on gathering. We rather quickly learned how to cultivate certain crops, such as wheat and barley, and thus adapted to farming. None of this happened overnight. The transition from hunter-gatherers to farmers who might occasionally hunt probably took a couple of generations or more, depending on the local environment. We know the first major transition took place in the hill country of the Fertile Crescent in the area between modern Iraq and Turkey. That area had an unusually high proportion of edible grains, good soil, and rain. We had already learned how to cook grains so they would become edible.

But once it became well established in a community, farming displaced the nomadic existence of hunter-gatherers. Farmers could settle down, and as they did so, the birth rate shot up, from one to three children per hunter-gatherer couple, to five or six or more. Nomadic mothers tended to breast feed their children until about age four, and during this period of lactation, women do not ovulate and thus cannot conceive and give birth. It was a natural form of birth control that was very necessary among nomads who had no means of transportation but their own backs.

Among settled farmers all that changed. The sudden increase in birth rates in turn became a new disruption to a stable environment. That disruption came gradually but it still triggered a new series of FROCA processes: new chaotic frontiers followed by new ecological releases that created new opportunities that got overexploited ending in various kinds of crashes. This sequence began about 10,000 years ago and ended about 6,000 years ago with the rise of the first ancient civilizations in Mesopotamia along the Tigris and Euphrates river valley. During this part of human cultural evolution, the typical human social order initially seems to have been hunter-gatherer egalitarianism with no formal leaders, and this persisted in the early period of garden agriculture. But as the agriculture expanded, so did population, and large populations put an end to small leaderless egalitarian communities. They were replaced, first in Mesopotamia, then along the Nile, later along the great river valleys of China and India, with urban societies supported by high-output riverine agriculture. In all these riverine civilizations in Asia and Africa, egalitarianism gave way to social orders marked by status hierarchies, despotism, and the rise of enormous social stratification. Moreover, all ancient civilizations in Eurasia, Africa, and the Americas depended on some form of slavery to do the heavy lifting. Many of these civilizations were god-king theocracies, or close to it. Most were what Jared Diamond calls "kleptocracies," by which he means the top social strata of society did almost no productive work but acquired nearly all the wealth. Those who did the most productive work (peasants, slaves, or serfs) got just enough to survive. (See Chapter 14 of Diamond's *Guns, Germs, and Steel*.)[4]

Diamond gives a clear account of how a growing population in the highly productive river valley drove this transition, as well as the causes underlying the change. Briefly, nomadic hunter-gatherers organized themselves in very small communities, rarely of more than 50 individuals. There was no storable wealth because, as nomads, they had to carry everything they had with them. All the members of the band shared kinship ties, knew each other well, and depended on each other to survive. Close interdependence, close bonds of kinship, and small numbers all combined to make a leaderless egalitarian social order an ideal survival strategy for primitive nomadic hunter-gatherers. But close bonds within the band were matched by suspicion of other bands not linked by kinship. That suspiciousness also helped survival in that it reduced the probability of turf battles between bands. Land was important because it took about 20 square kilometers or more, depending on the environment, climate, etc., to feed one nomadic hunter-gatherer. A band of 30 thus needed an average feeding range of about 600 square kilometers. Thus the nomadic human population had to be, and was, well spread out.

Such large ranges made it relatively simple for humans to avoid clashes, but it also meant that strangers were regarded as potential threats. Shifting to hillside garden farming did not at first threaten our egalitarian ways, but before long, the now settled population began growing rapidly as the birth rate shot up. Communities grew from bands of 20 to 40 people to settled villages of 200 or more. Then villages began to cluster as the geometric expansion continued. At this point, anarchy began to threaten for several related reasons. First, farming now produced storable wealth for the first time, raising the question of how the surplus was to be shared. Second, the larger populations created communities less bound to each other by close kinship ties and mutual interdependence. Enforcing rules to resolve disputes among members of the community became more difficult. This situation led to often bloody fights, feuds, and chaos, and it threatened to lapse into anarchy. It soon became clear that something had to be done.

The first step was to elect a part-time "head man" commissioned to resolve disputes and avoid violence. That solution worked in small communities but as communities got larger, a part-timer without authority to enforce decisions could no longer cope. The solution was to elect a full-time chief, with limited enforcement authority. But as the population grew, new villages arose to house the same community now large enough to form tribes and clans. The weak chief had to become a strong chief and also had to have help, other full-time people to act as sub-chiefs and to help perform other duties. Thus began what we now call a government and a civil service. It was also the beginning of an aristocratic class, taxation, and theocracy and a formal priesthood.

Chiefs, at this stage, had become so powerful that the election of a new chief became a major cause of fierce factional rivalries. The same solution appeared almost everywhere: the chief's position became hereditary. That shift was the beginning of royal families while the strong hereditary chief's subordinates became nobles. Both the royal family and the nobles acquired special status and special privileges denied to common folks. Policies were no longer made by councils of elders; the chief and his nobles began setting down the law, effectively establishing a kleptocracy, as Diamond defined it: a government controlled by the upper classes that acquire most of the wealth. The lower classes who supply the labor and produce most of the largely agricultural wealth barely subsist. This gradual transition from egalitarianism to despotism was an extended process of adaptation, one that had to create a method of containing anarchy and reducing chaos. It may not have been fair, but it was successful in creating and maintaining a new equilibrium. One of most important ways that despotic governments maintain social equilibrium is inhibiting innovation both in technology and in culture. All the technology necessary to create and sustain civilization was in place before cities got large enough to qualify as civilization. These include the substitution of bronze for stone in tools and weapons, the wheel and wheeled vehicles, the domestication of animals, and pictographic writing. For the next 5,000 years, very little else truly new was invented. The major exceptions were iron tools and weapons, and the alphabet, around 1,000 BCE. Not until some time after the fall of Rome would a new age of innovation begin in Western Europe.

All this has important implications for our immediate post-2008 future. One way or the other, equilibrium constrains what we think of as freedom, and that includes the freedom both to innovate and to compete. Innovation and competition are both agents of change and in the punctuation phase give the process of evolution its dynamic. But part of that dynamic is to get back to equilibrium, and that requires competition and innovation to be constrained.

For the last 500-odd years, punctuation has dominated the world as the explosion of post-Roman innovations lifted Western Europe first out of the post-crash Middle Ages, into the more dynamic feudal ages and finally into the Age of Enlightenment. The collapse of Rome's central authority destroyed a major constraint on innovation in good part by politically fragmenting Europe. The collapse of central authority opened the door—gave ecological release—to would-be innovators and entrepreneurs. Political fragmentation assured that local feudal despotisms were forced to adopt innovations such as artillery used by rivals to threaten the despot's power. They might well have preferred to quash such innovations, and in fact just that happened in both China and Japan. China and Japan were both centralized despotisms not fragmented by geography. China, in fact, had enjoyed a technological advantage over Western Europe from shortly after Rome fell until about AD 1500. Only in the twenty-first century can it be said that China has regained a degree of technological parity with the West, and that only after China dropped most of the constraints imposed by communism and adopted a version of capitalism.[5]

Among the critical innovations of the late Middle Ages and Renaissance that lifted Western Europe from a backwater civilization to world domination were the adaptation of Chinese gunpowder to artillery and other firearms, the printing press, the telescope and microscope, the clock, square-rigged sailing ships with sternpost rudders, and a number of navigation instruments beginning with the compass. All these were disruptive of the old order in many different ways and in effect created one new FROCA frontier after another. Each came with its own version of boom and bust. Each new innovation would also create new problems, often enough solved with yet other innovations. Despotic kings and god-kings had been the standard form of governance in agricultural economies. As these new innovations brought forth the industrial revolution as well as new and higher standards of mass literacy, the democratic nation state began to emerge, challenging the preeminence of hereditary domains under the rule of monarchs by "divine right." Under despotic governments, the idea of personal rights protected by the government plays almost no role. Instead, in the interest of maintaining law, order, and stability, despotic governments focus on, and try to enforce, a list of personal obligations. Despotisms can range from the cruel, such as Stalin's, to the relatively benign—say that of Elizabeth I of England. But whether cruel or benign, the big job is to maintain stability. Indeed, stability has to be the primary goal of almost any government of whatever system or scale. The same holds true for almost any large organization as well. A corporation, for example, has a legal duty to preserve shareholder value, and that usually means keeping things as stable as possible. Hierarchical control and heavy constraints on internal competition have a proven record of keeping an organization internally stable. Such stability also generally inhibits innovation, which itself can be internally disruptive. It is often noted that natural ecologies are almost always "self-organized," that is, there is no hierarchical management to maintain equilibrium. But such self-organization is usually expressed as a balance of power among the competitors and that balance is what maintains equilibrium. Such a balance comes more as a result of exhaustion and the end of the FROCA process. The weaker forces in the competitive struggle have lost out, but none of the stronger survivors can displace the others. The result is a balance of power that emerges naturally with deliberation playing no part in it.

Among humans, however, deliberation often does play a part in bringing about an ecological balance of power. In an economic ecology, exhausted competitors often make agreements to limit competition, an arrangement usually called a cartel. Even if cartels are illegal, as they are in the United States for the most part, business firms still make informal or unwritten agreements to limit competition in price, business hours, or services offered.

Cartels aim to limit competition in order to achieve market equilibrium and stability. Authoritarian hierarchies aim to achieve a stable equilibrium within a company. Together, these two strategies produce equilibrium within an economic ecosystem, but such stability also results in what we have come to think of as economic stagnation. We are caught in a bind in that we need constant growth to remain dynamically stable at something close to full employment. Constant growth depends on continuous innovation to create new industries that drive growth. Thus a growing economy will have some proportion of the work force employed in the growth sector. Should growth cease, under our system of labor employment, workers will be laid off, which is both painful to those workers and their families and communities, and politically threatening to the party in power. Thus both conservatives and liberals usually claim to support growth.

Today, however, we refer more and more to "sustainable" growth because we are beginning to see that constant growth creates problems of its own. We begin to run out of natural resources or drive up their prices much faster than inflation. Pollution becomes a mounting problem, putting growth as such under an ecological cloud.

Each new growth industry experiences its own FROCA process. It begins with an innovation that creates a new frontier of growth. If the innovation provides "greater fitness" for some segment of the market it grows rapidly. And it will continue to grow as long as the quality gets better and costs come down at the same time. But that compounding process can go on only so long, and at some point, better quality begins to cost more, not less. When that happens, growth slows sharply, and the industry typically finds itself with too much capacity. Output suddenly drops from growth plus replacement demand to replacement demand only. That happened to the auto industry in late 1929. Output promptly fell from 5 million vehicles a year to about 2.5 million, a 50 percent drop. Many firms failed and all were forced to cut way back.

So, what kind of a post-crash economy do we want now, as we head into the second decade of the twenty-first century? As I write this, in the fall of 2009, the collapse has ended and the stock market has regained some of its loss. Unemployment, however, continues to rise, and here we come to a crunch issue. As I have noted earlier in the book, 2008 came at the end of an extended period of growth in consumer spending. Much of that growth in spending was fueled by increasing debt at the expense of saving. Any forecast that envisions a return to consumer spending at 2006 levels and above is not realistic unless the federal government is somehow going to stimulate another major spending binge on credit. If they do, that will only make the crisis that much worse.

But we will defer most of this discussion to Chapter 11.

NOTES

1. See Eldredge, Niles. *The Pattern of Evolution.* New York: W. H. Freeman, 1999.

2. Wallace, William McDonald. *Techno-Cultural Evolution: Cycles of Creation and Conflict.* Dulles, VA: Potomac Books, 2006.

3. Hauser, Marc. *The Evolution of Communication.* Cambridge: MIT Press, 1999.

4. Diamond, Jared. *Guns, Germs, and Steel: The Fate of Human Society.* New York: Norton, 1999. Chapter 14 (From Egalitarianism to Kleptocracy) is devoted to describing this process.

5. I first visited China in 1970 and changes evident by 2005 when I made an extended trip were almost mind-boggling. China's major cities at lease had seemed to jump from the early nineteenth century directly into the twenty-first century in a single bound once released from the tight bounds of early communism.

Chapter 10

HUMAN BEHAVIOR IN PUNCTUATION VERSUS EQUILIBRIUM

Soldiers behave differently in combat than they do in garrison duty. In garrison, if they want to get promoted, soldiers follow the rules closely and tend to go by the book. Garrison duty, of course, is usually rather stable and has a large repertoire of standard solutions to commonly encountered problems; in other words, it amounts to "equilibrium." Combat, however, compares to a "punctuation" period. Soldiers must react quickly and deal spontaneously and off-the-cuff with unexpected and unplanned-for events in an often chaotic situation. When garrison soldiers are caught off guard by an unexpected surprise attack, the solutions embedded in "the book" may well not apply.

By the same token, people who work in start-up firms behave differently than do the people who work in large, well established and successful firms. The latter typically pay close attention to following the rules and regulations. The folks in start-ups, on the other hand, may be breaking new ground and struggling daily with survival. They are in "combat," so to speak, and may well be adhering to Vince Lombardi's dictum, "Winning isn't the main thing, it's the only thing." It is the only thing that counts because in those circumstances, you often must win simply to survive. The old Etonian motto is much better advice for people living and working in an equilibrium environment: "It isn't whether you win or lose, it's how you play the game." Be a good sport. Follow the rules. If you lose, lose graciously. Congratulate the winner. If you do win, be magnanimous to the losers. Let them save face, and do not gloat about winning.

Most of us will see Etonian behavior as an ideal we all might aspire to, and in equilibrium it surely is. But that behavior and the values behind it are of little use in times of all-out competition to survive. Here, the nice, Etonian good sport is likely to finish last. On the opposite side, we often see that, in an equilibrium environment, those who follow Vince Lombardi's ethic finish last. Consider Winston Churchill and George Patton. Churchill was a disaster as a peacetime politician in the twenties. But the very behavior that marginalized Churchill in times of peace quite literally saved Britain in its darkest hour in the summer of 1940. His physical courage, absolute determination to win, and relentless energy carried Britain through to win the Battle of Britain when most of the people in his government, including King George VI and Lord Halifax, would have preferred to make a deal with Hitler.

Today we might even say Churchill was deep in denial after Dunkirk. Despite the loss of much of the English army's weapons and the collapse of its only ally, France, Churchill denied Britain had clearly lost the war. Most other nations and many Americans—including our Ambassador to Britain, Joseph Kennedy—were all convinced Britain was finished. But with his fierce competitive spirit and refusal to give up even after serious defeats, Churchill ultimately won the day. On the other hand, those very same behaviors brought Churchill to grief time and again as a politician in peacetime (and at Etonian-like schools in his youth).[1]

One of the most interesting insights D'Este brings to us is how much the Etonian peacetime ethic had permeated Britain's high command in the army and navy. That ethic rendered them psychologically helpless when confronting Hitler and his Vince Lombardi-type generals. Britain's brass had spent peacetime worrying about their cricket scores and being gracious, perfect gentlemen at social events. Their German counterparts were learning from their loss in World War I and busy crafting new tactics and technology and cultivating a winning ethic. It caught the British and French flat-footed in the spring of 1940, although in terms of tanks, planes, and divisions the two sides were evenly matched. It took Churchill, despite his many personality quirks and frequent bad judgments, to save Britain after the catastrophe at Dunkirk in June 1940. He not only energized England with speeches but he also quashed the Etonian ethic in the British military. That made him unpopular with the military brass, but as Churchill saw Britain's interests, "winning was not the main thing it was the only thing that mattered."

The case of Patton is similar, in reverse. As a wartime general, he distinguished himself brilliantly. But after the war ended, Patton proved a disaster in peacetime. His battlefield élan poorly equipped him for the restrained, carefully balanced sphere of diplomacy.

In business we have long observed a similar dichotomy. The entrepreneur who does well founding a start-up and guiding it to dominance in its field often does poorly after that success when it comes to managing the successful company day to day. On the other hand, the cautious and meticulous administrator, who can manage a large company very well, often would not know how to get a start-up going.

This behavioral dichotomy creates an ethical dilemma for those who are expected to perform, say, in the competitive rat race of punctuation, but who are being judged by Etonian rules of equilibrium. And of course the reverse is equally true. Those born and bred to follow the rules in an equilibrium atmosphere that honors tradition and obedience to the rules often look down on fierce competitors as not being "gentlemen." Churchill was long tarred with that brush and kept on the back benches until the war started. Again, the officer who was always a pain in the ass while in garrison often does very well in combat. He does not hesitate to toss out "the book" when he realizes it has no answers to the problems in an unexpected crisis. This can be true of both officers and enlisted men.

We see this different orientation between punctuation and equilibrium in bold relief when comparing American to Middle Eastern Islamic culture. It is a classic clash between a culture of personal rights and the freedom to innovate on one hand and a traditional culture that clings with great passion to the "divinely revealed truth of the Holy Koran." The Koran spells out a God-given law called Sharia. For Muslims who truly believe their scripture, they must conclude that the West is run by infidels who flaunt God's sacred law. To the true believer, the idea of a democracy passing man-made laws clearly reveals the Western infidel's sacrilegious arrogance. They have the audacity to brag about man-made laws often in direct contradiction of God's divinely revealed laws.

Not all Muslims and perhaps not even a majority of Muslims take the Koran as literal truth. Many have never even read it. Yet the true believers control the "authorized" interpretation of the Koran and other scripture and they dominate the education of the young. They occupy the high theological ground and are almost never openly challenged by the skeptics within Islam. And of course there are Christians and Jews who also believe in God's revealed truth, and God as the lawgiver. But the true believers definitely cannot impose their views on Christian or Jewish scriptural skeptics. In the West, the secularists control the high ideological moral ground, and most Western education is based on science, not scripture. Islam is nowhere near reaching that point.

Unfortunately, American culture and its economy is a lively, even chaotic mixture of punctuation and equilibrium. The punctuation side has been dominant for over 200 years. Yet pockets of equilibrium are found everywhere at the subcultural level. Some people live in both worlds at the same time. Some are able to tailor their behavior and make appropriate behavioral adjustments. For example, some soldiers go between garrison life and active combat with relative ease, but many others do not. Broadly speaking, people living within subcultural equilibrium soon find their subculture favors protecting tradition with strict rules of behavior and resisting change. The broader culture of punctuation, however, celebrates change as the royal road to progress toward something better.

Let us look at how these behaviors played out in the financial sector leading up to 2008. What we can note is that after 1980 the financial sector was no longer in post-1929 equilibrium. It was no longer following the Etonian rules of ethics. Instead it shifted progressively to a new punctuated frontier and it began following Vince Lombardi's dictum of "winning [in this case more money] is the only thing." This was not done openly. Indeed most of the rhetoric continued to uphold the Etonian rules even while actual behavior shifted ever more toward Vince Lombardi. Greed soon trumped the gentlemanly ethics of "playing the game according to the rules" of fiduciary responsibility to clients. Very quickly actual behavior shifted to winning as much as possible as quickly as possible in the various highly leveraged get-rich-quick schemes deregulation had opened up. Not only bankers, but lawyers, accountants, bond rating companies, trust funds, and others saw and exploited this rapid relaxation of the rules to the point where Bernie Madoff could launch a Ponzi scheme that bilked many billions of dollars out of thousands of investors, including charities.

Lenders embraced the rapid relaxation of ethics once they saw they could collect mortgage fees up front. They could then sell off their mortgage loans along with the risk of default to others. The others would in turn sell off the risk they had taken on by "securitizing" the loans and then selling off packages of that debt. They did that not only with mortgages, but with credit card debt, auto loans, and other such debt. All debt was increasingly "securitized." Economists often applaud such innovative practices because they make credit more available, flexible, and mobile.

Economists and bankers often ignore the huge moral hazard involved. Those financial innovations played a major role in creating the debt bubble along a wide variety of fronts. They also undermined a fundamental sense of fiduciary trust, which, in turn, negated the ethic to minimize risk to bank depositors whose funds were used to make mortgage loans. If the bank could sell off the loan— and its risk—both the depositors and the banks seemed to be off the hook. Ah, here is where moral hazard again rears its ugly head. Before deregulation, when banks usually lived off the interest of their mortgages, they had a practical incentive to make sure the borrowers were creditworthy. Now the incentive was reversed: because the risk seemed to be gone, it paid to make as many loans as possible. Credit standards were immediately relaxed, all the way to the No Income, No Job or Assets NINJA loans. "Bad Credit?" some ads asked. "Having credit problems only proves you're human. Come to us. We can get you a loan." Predatory lending soon became the name of the game. Tens of thousands of borrowers were seduced into getting loans they could not possibly pay back. It is okay to claim individual lenders were behaving unethically, they were indeed. But such guilt-tripping is pointless unless one addresses, and in fact changes, the policies that gave rise to the predatory behavior. In fact it is worse than pointless because it makes it seem a lapse of personal ethics was at fault when that lapse was virtually engineered by deregulation.

There is a new but growing concern that the Obama Administration is not really planning to reregulate the financial sector very much. That may yet change, but in his speech on the first anniversary of the failure of Lehman Brothers, Obama chastised Wall Street for personal greed during the period leading up to the 2008 collapse. He gave no hint, however, that he was planning to remove the post-1980 incentives that gave rise to and even justified that greed. At this writing, the proposed changes in financial sector regulations are little more than restatements of the powers possessed by the government after deregulation and do not come close to preventing a repeat of the meltdown of 2008.

People, and all other forms of life, respond to actual incentives, positive or negative. For humans, regulations usually embody incentives. And yes, the regulation has yet to be invented that some people will not try to game by finding a loophole or some other way to get around it. And of course the more complex and restrictive the regulations, the more opportunities for gaming will arise. To work well, in other words, regulations cannot be too little or too much. Too few regulations beget competitive chaos, and too many complex regulations beget red tape stagnation, which ultimately begets a new chaos of massive gaming to get around it.

Innovations in technology account for both cultural change and economic growth, as we have stressed. Each new technology triggers the FROCA process by opening up new frontiers for competitive opportunities that subsequently get overexploited and then crash. An adaptation then follows as the new technology "matures" and stabilizes. Our behavior changes, as we have stressed, depending on where we are in the process. But as one innovation in technology piles onto others, we create a rich mixture of cultural pockets in various stages of growth or maturity. That is, they are either in the punctuation phase of change or the equilibrium phase of stability.

As we have shown, the two sets of behaviors are often at odds with each other. The punctuation phase features a highly competitive frontier where to survive we must win and beat our rivals. Adaptation to equilibrium, on the other hand, requires muted competition. Constraints on competition thus require low levels of change enforced by stern requirements to maintain traditions and follow the rules. Conforming to the rules is all-important. It is not whether you win or lose, but how you play the game that counts in equilibrium.

Evolution thus places us in a rich, but often highly confusing mixture of cultural standards. Internally, these different standards often lead to political gridlock when, for example, the issue is government economic and social policies to handle medical insurance. Externally, these different standards can and have led to a clash of civilizations such as between the secular West and Islamic fundamentalism.

So the question arises: Has evolution placed us in an acute dilemma? Are we now, in the post-2008 period, facing a choice we cannot or do not want to make? If we continue with democratic government based on innovative freedom and *laissez-faire*, will we open the door to more unacceptable chaos and new bubbles that burst? Has capitalism's long-noted tendency toward creative destruction evolved to the point where it is mostly destruction and little good creation? If the answers are yes, then are we forced to return to a highly authoritarian government (in our case most likely fascist)?

Authoritarian governments can constrain competition and enforce traditions very well. They can suppress internal innovation just as easily. In fact, authoritarian governments evolved precisely to end the chaos and anarchy of egalitarianism once population growth was no longer constrained by nomadic hunter-gatherer ecologies. But authoritarian governments also tend to become highly stratified social hierarchies. These in turn tend to become kleptocracies where the upper classes, which have all the power, richly reward themselves. They tend to keep the lower orders at close to the poverty level. It took democracies based on personal rights (including the freedom to innovate) to bring an end to all that. But, as we have seen, that merely triggered a new FROCA sequence.

So, is there a third way? Can we devise a system that constrains competition within democratic parameters and yet allows for controlled innovation? The answer is yes, and we have already invented it. It is called free enterprise. However, in 1929 and again in 2008, we nearly allowed casino capitalism to destroy it. We think of capitalism and free enterprise as synonymous, but they are not. Capitalism subordinates labor to capital; free enterprise brings labor in as an equal partner. That eliminates internal kleptocracy within the firm. To preserve free enterprise, we must first reregulate the financial sector. Those regulations need to keep that sector locked in equilibrium and held to a firm ethic of fiduciary responsibility with leverage well constrained. Those policies will abolish casino capitalism. Wall Street will fiercely resist that abolition to be sure. But the Wall Street kleptocrats will no longer call the shots. Regulations that firmly distinguish between fair and unfair practices must also be established to put reasonable constraints on competition. One of the great failings of economic pseudoscience was the fiction that fairness was a value judgment that had no place in economic science. Within companies made up of equal partners, the new ethic will be "competition among companies, cooperation within them." Partnership between capital and labor makes that possible.

Again we already know how to do all this. We just have not quite got it right, yet. Our final chapter will show how we can get it right. It will show how we can adjust economic theory and business ethics to establish an economic ecology based on a sustainable system of free enterprise.[2]

NOTES

1. D'Este, Carlo. *Warlord: A Life of Winston Churchill at War, 1874–1945*. New York: HarperCollins, 2008.

2. Wallace, William McDonald. *Techno-Cultural Evolution: Cycles of Creation and Conflict*. Dulles, VA: Potomac Books, 2006.

Part III

THE POST-CRASH OUTLOOK

Chapter 11

GETTING IT RIGHT

I t takes a good deal of trial and error to get things right. That is certainly true
in economics. Yet we will learn a lot faster if we are *prepared and willing* to
learn from actual experience. We learn by making mistakes, but it takes a whole
lot longer if we are misled by passionate beliefs in false ideologies and ignore our
mistakes. Passions and inaccuracies often go together. In our economic and
political affairs, false theory and ideological passion frequently tempt us to dismiss
actual experience when it conflicts with our pet theories and ideologies. We dismiss
such contrary experience as anomalies we can safely ignore.

So if we want to get these things right, we first need to clear away the wreck-
age of the past by bringing theory and ideology into the coherent reality of actual
experience. Then trial and error can lead to real progress.

This book has focused on three areas where experience has been ignored by
our theories and ideologies, right left and center. The first area deals with how
the FROCA process of evolution (punctuated equilibrium) governs boom and
bust and has thus shaped the alternation of change and stability in our social lives
and political economies. None of our theories or ideologies even addresses the
issue of change and stability as a process of evolution.

The second area deals with labor in our industrial sector and how we depend
mostly on hired labor with its rigid unit costs. Such dependence creates needless
instability and unemployment drives us, in turn, to strive for continual economic
growth to avoid unacceptable unemployment. That growth is now beginning to
cause serious environmental damage. Again, mainstream theory and ideology on
the right, the left, and center all support economic growth. They differ mainly on
the best way to achieve it. No position truly embraces the most straightforward
alternative of combining capital and labor into a corporate partnership where
capital and labor share both profit and losses together.

The third major concern deals with whether government should participate in
the management of the economy and if so, how. Here theories and ideologies span
the spectrum from not at all (*laissez-faire*) on the right to total control (Marxism)
on the left. A middle ground does exist of course, but one unenlightened by the

real process of evolution or of the pathology of the adversarial relationship between capital and labor.

Let us begin by looking at the process of evolution. Our biology, of course, is mostly determined by the process of natural selection of random mutations, more or less as laid out by Darwin. Random events also influence cultural evolution but the many different human cultures that have evolved owe much more to conscious selection by humans. Consider the approach to government in various cultures. Variations of bottom-up democracy and of top-down authoritarianism and theocracies all reflect consciously chosen responses to many different environments and ecological conditions. Our free enterprise system evolved by conscious choice, but from the bottom up and in response to the new freedom to innovate that followed the collapse of Rome's central authority. All economic systems can be thought of as software that specifies how a society will operate its evolving technology and even whether or not to allow innovations to continue. Technology can of course be influenced by random events, but it is far more driven by conscious innovation. Yet, just as with our computers, the specifics of both hardware and software owe much to trial and error. Trial and error must cope with an ever-changing environment driven by the boom and bust of the FROCA process. As I have stressed in this book, economic, social, political, and cultural evolution are all driven by innovations in technology including the software changes new hardware may require. Significant changes in the hardware usually require changes in the software that spell out how society engages with the hardware. Those changes lead to different cultures. For example, capitalism and communism are alternative systems of "software" for similar industrial technologies, and they define quite different cultures, social values, and political systems for the broader culture, often leading to deep conflict. Again, our earlier theories and ideologies did not pick up the realities of FROCA because of Darwin's uniformitarianism. All of them had reached their present levels of misconception by the time our theories of physics took actual experience into account and laid uniformitarianism to rest.

So, given FROCA, can we achieve a fair balance between punctuation and equilibrium? That is to say, can we achieve a balance between freedom and authoritarianism? Can we achieve sustainable growth without bubbles, destructive crashes, or an environmental crisis? If so, can we also achieve that balance without stagnation? The remainder of this book addresses these questions. If we get it right, the answer to all of them is: "Yes we can." The trick to getting it right first requires building upon what we already know works. Second it is necessary to get rid of policies that we know do not work. But again, to do that we need to get rid of the false theories that sustain and even justify those policies. We often continue to practice what does not work because theory or ideology suggests it should. Too often we avoid doing what does work for want of support in either theory or ideology.

So let us now turn to our second major concern, namely the way ideology and theory tells us we should employ labor. Here, liberals and conservatives share a set of blinders. Both assume that in the corporate sector employees should work, not in partnership with capital, but as hirelings. Hirelings, of course, work in a subordinated position to the employer. Marx, remember, was highly critical of the fact that labor was subordinated and then exploited. It was thus surprising to me to learn that one of the first pronouncements Lenin made in 1918 upon taking over as head of the of the new communist state was this: "All citizens will immediately become hired employees of the State." At a stroke, labor under communism was subordinated to the employer exactly as it was under capitalism. In fact, it was far worse because workers became in effect, industrial serfs. Under capitalism, a worker could quit one employer and go to work for another. Or workers could freely join together and form a partnership with others.

Western liberals never went as far as Lenin, but they did not disavow his approach. Indeed, even milder socialists put labor in a subordinated status as hirelings. So did trade unions, formed to protect workers from capitalist exploitation. Unions would have no point under corporate partnership. So once formed, trade unions developed a vested interest in keeping labor subordinated to justify their existence. Neoclassical liberals then favored hired labor in good part because the unions did. For their part, capitalists, who often started out as small partnerships, tended to expand with hired labor, not by adding partners. Why? No doubt in part, the owners wanted to avoid sharing growth in profits, or put another way, to avoid diluting their equity. But there was more to it than that.

In previous books I showed how Britain's enclosure movement created great social distance between owners and laborers just as capitalism began to emerge "from the bottom up." Enclosure itself aimed to rationalize British agriculture. A major feature of it was to enclose lands previously under tillage by tenant farmers into pastureland for sheep. As a result thousands upon thousands of tenant farmers were displaced and became rural refugees. They had nowhere to go except into cities where there were no jobs. Many turned to crime and drink. Families fell apart, mothers handed infant children over to local orphanages—children often afflicted with malnutrition and fetal alcohol syndrome. The orphanages were short of funds and none too compassionate and so orphanages often mistreated their charges. At age 15, the males were turned out into the street, usually hating authority of any kind. Often enough, they ended up engaged in crime as portrayed by Charles Dickens in *Oliver Twist*.

By 1700 these rural refugees and their offspring began to constitute a new underclass, the proletarians, who became the core of the British working class, supplying the labor for the industrial revolution. But the social distance between this urban proletariat and the rising middle class, often called bourgeoisie, was now very great. These progeny of once stalwart farmers acquired a reputation as drunken scum, lazy, and untrustworthy. For middle-class business owners to form partnerships with such workers was socially unimaginable.

But that was then and this is now. We have learned that partnership can, in fact, tolerate social distance and ethnic differences if not too extreme. The reason is that partners agree, first to pursue a common goal, and second, to share fairly both in the rewards of success in good times and in the pain of hard times. Hard times are much easier to take when shared because the sharing eliminates the privation and humiliation that come with layoffs.

Consider how partnership would automatically put a damper on management greed. First, if a few members got multi-million dollar bonuses during a downturn while the bulk of the other partners got cuts in pay or benefits, the other partners would probably revolt. Such greed would clearly violate all sense of fairness. Partnership does not mean that everyone gets equal pay, nor even equal pay for equal work. Rather pay would be a function of how much the different partners have invested in the partnership and how much they bring in terms of skill, experience, and education. Outstanding performance by particular individuals can of course be recognized. For example, if certain individuals consistently perform far better than average, their pay grade could rise at a faster rate than average. Recognition could also come in the form of nonmonetary awards, certificates, or benefits. The equity principle for hired labor is equal pay for equal jobs. For partners or stockholders, the equity principle holds that equal investments should receive equal sums. Thus every share of common stock gets precisely the same rate of return. The difference in income between partners reflects differing levels of investment by them.

On the upswing or downswing, partners share according to their relative rank or pay grade, which reflects their relative levels of investment in the enterprise. On a downswing, everyone's pay rate will drop, but the partners will remain employed unless the firm goes under. Flexible rates of pay allow firms to cut prices to maintain demand. If firms rely on hirelings, pay rates must remain at contracted-for levels and that keeps unit labor cost as rigid as interest rates. Rigid labor costs make it difficult to lower prices in a slump, and instead encourage or necessitate laying off workers. Many a company has gone bankrupt by relying too much on debt so as not to dilute per share earnings when things are going well. Come a downturn, they are caught by surprise. They cannot reduce the interest rates agreed to, and so, if they cannot service the debt, they must declare bankruptcy. The vulnerability is the same when a company relies excessively on cost-rigid wage labor.

Hired labor, in short, destabilizes the macro economy. Actually, this is true even in classical theory. Rigid wage costs negate the key premise of Say's Law of Markets that supply creates its own demand. J. B. Say insisted that unit labor costs must be flexible so that prices can fall in a slump and he was clear on this point. Given flexible costs, a company can cut prices instead of laying off labor. If partnership is widely practiced, employment will then be far more stable. Indeed, this flexibility was part of the original justification for *laissez-faire*, which assumed that supply would create its own demand. But again, supply will create its own demand and keep employment reasonably stable only if unit labor costs remain flexible with downside elasticity in case of a slump. Much of the failure of *laissez-faire* arises from insisting it works just as well with cost-rigid hired labor. It does not. In my view, had conservatives been clear about this and promoted partnership, we would not have had a Great Depression in 1929. (I documented my case that partnership could have avoided the 1929–1940 Great Depression.[1]) And in that event, we would have had far less need of a welfare state. We would also have avoided the Keynesian fix that philosophically opened the door to run-away consumer misuse of credit. But greed to avoid sharing profits was in my view a main reason capitalists wanted to stick with hired labor despite the adversarial relationship and its rigid costs. Indeed, one can imagine Lenin's motive was in principle the same, but to avoid sharing power with labor. Lenin wanted all control in the hands of the Politburo.

A related labor policy issue concerns how we handle government expenses in a downturn, especially the wages of civil servants and transfer payments to welfare recipients. In principle, it is possible to relate these expenses to the revenue available to pay for them at least within reasonable limits. Doing so would reduce the need to lay off government employees on one hand while handing out stimulus payments to create jobs on the other.

The third area of concern deals with how much, if at all, government should regulate the economy. I have discussed at length how the conservative passion for *laissez-faire* on the right and the liberal passion for political correctness on the left combined to bring about the crash of 2008. Before going further, let me point out that had we gotten it right about the FROCA process in boom and bust, and also about the logic of depending more on partnership than on hirelings in staffing the industrial revolution, the government's role would be less controversial.

But that was not the way it was, and it is no use grieving about it now. So the question for today is: What regulations do we need now, given the legacy of the past? Before we begin, however, we need to note the post-crash Wall Street revival of the case for doing little or nothing.

One well-respected consulting economist, Nariman Behravesh, for example published a book in 2009 entitled *Spin-Free Economics*.[2] Behravesh says much that makes sense in general, but unfortunately most of his discussion about financial regulation does not. Many of his clients are on Wall Street. Thus he gives the conventional justification for financial deregulation and for unregulated hedge funds and private equity funds so beloved by Wall Street. Behravesh begins this section of his book by stating:

> After every financial crisis, there is a call for tighter regulation. The subprime crisis of 2007 and 2008 is no exception. Nonetheless the calls are at odds with the large benefits that have accrued to the United States and other countries that have deregulated their financial markets in the last few decades.[3]

Behravesh implicitly assumes rational behavior to make that case. Yes, the appearance of large benefits seemed to be the case up to about 2006 or 2007. But then many of those benefits began to vanish into thin air. What Behravesh ignores is how unconstrained leverage ignites irresistible attacks of irrational exuberance that induces Wall Street greed whenever leveraged bubbles form. Behravesh takes these bubbles as a normal part of economic life. He says that not much can be done about them.

Irrational exuberance negates many of the advantages of a bubble by causing it to burst and always has. If regulations constrain leverage, as they did for 40 years after the Great Depression, bubbles do not form and investors do not get irrationally exuberant. Behravesh ignores completely how that stable 40-odd-year period of a well-regulated (and thus very stable) financial sector accommodated all the financing needs of that era. It accommodated welfare and public works deficits during the Great Depression. It then accommodated the huge deficits needed to finance World War II. Then, to the surprise of many, it easily handled all the credit needs of the postwar boom that lasted from 1950 to 1972. All that success came without a single credit crunch of any kind, no bursting bubbles, and very low unemployment after the war. The boom itself ended with the OPEC oil-price crisis that began in 1973.

Recall Behravesh's opening statement quoted earlier, cautioning against financial re-regulation. He takes credit for the gains made by leverage, but ignores the fact that bursting bubbles later wiped out many or even most of these gains. Moreover, one of those so-called gains simply made it possible to gain easier access to credit. That can be a good thing of course, but also a bad thing. Such "gains" led directly to the largest explosion of corporate and consumer debt in history. When the bubble burst, the assets that served as the collateral for the debt turned out to be the same assets that had vaporized when the bubble burst. Suddenly, many investors were upside down. The gains they thought they had made were gone but the debt that had financed those transient gains was still around, leading directly to the ruin of many.[4]

Behravesh argues that "despite having a bad reputation, debt securitization has been a good thing on balance."[5] He then points out that in 1985 one-third of the $1.5 trillion in U.S. mortgages had been securitized, that is, bundled into packages and sold as investments. By 2006, he happily notes, the value of mortgages had risen to $10 trillion of which three quarters had been securitized. It apparently escaped Behravesh that it was the very success of securitization that not only enabled the subprime mortgage bubble to form, but also actively encouraged its formation. For the first time, lenders could make money from bad loans—if they sold off the bad loan together with its risk of default and kept the profits. While Behravesh admits such loans were problematic, he betrays no awareness of the moral hazard securitization induced. If a lender can make money from the fees and other charges associated with making bad loans to people he knows cannot pay off, he will do so when he knows he avoids the risk of default. Motivated by profit, lenders will make risk-free subprime loans as often as possible.

If such predatory loans pose a danger to economic stability, then regulations should preclude them. If you do not want ducks hunted in a certain area, you do not open the gate to hunters with shotguns and then just tell them not to shoot the ducks.

Behravesh also leaps to the defense of unregulated hedge funds, private equity funds, and sovereign wealth funds. He quotes Charlie McCreevy, the European Union's Internal Market Commissioner, who said, "Hedge funds and private equity funds are good for the market. They have given greater liquidity, have added shareholder value and they have helped rationalization and innovation of companies."[6]

Behravesh points out these funds hardly existed in 1981, but by 2006 there were 6,500 of them, controlling (at that time) $1.5 trillion in assets. He does not mention that, by late 2008, a large proportion of those assets were subprime mortgage bundles considered toxic, that is, worthless.[7] So much for shareholder value from financial deregulation. Even so, his bottom-line statement is: "In the final analysis the benefits provided by the hedge funds are greater than the moderately low risks they pose for the financial system." First, most of the benefits mentioned went mainly to fund managers who collected huge, largely untaxed bonuses before the 2008 collapse. Some managers—George Soros is a good example—made billions. On the other hand, many thousands of employees lost their jobs in "meat axe" rationalizations by take-over artists who collected hundreds of millions for their trouble.

As 2008 proved, the free enterprise system nearly collapsed from leveraged speculation releasing rampant greed thanks to the deregulation Wall Street is again rushing to defend. In late 2008, unconstrained greed had been fully revealed for the destructive force it was. But now greed is fighting back. At this writing, the Obama Administration is backing off from one financial reform under pressure from Wall Street and economists like Behravesh. In 2009, during the summer Congressional recess, Wall Street lobbyists by the score descended on Congressional Democrats and tried with some success to convince them to back off.[8]

Neoclassical economists began writing learned think pieces explaining just how useful all those financial innovations and derivatives really had been.

Some argue passionately about keeping the government from regulating the salaries and bonuses of Wall Street companies that failed and had to be rescued. First the claim is made that it would be unconstitutional, but then, in the view of many, so was the rescue money. Second, they claim the government could not do it well, and in any event has no business trying to cap payments to management. Well, the government has always set pay caps to earnings by civil servants, elected officials, and for the whole military. Third, the argument goes that if the government does limit earnings, then all that brilliant Wall Street talent will go abroad, to Britain, Bahrain, Singapore, or elsewhere. Perhaps, if the folks who destroyed our financial sector were to flee abroad, the nation would be better off. If the top management at companies such as Lehman Brothers, Bear Stearns, Merrill Lynch, Washington Mutual, Citibank, Wachovia, Countrywide, Fannie Mae, Freddie Mac, and other losers were to rush overseas, the United States should declare a day of national Thanksgiving for our deliverance. These guys may have had high levels of academic intelligence, but they still did not have a clue. They were flat out incompetent when it came to assessing actual financial risk. Why ever should we fear if they decided to leave?

Another major misconception here is that these obscene, kleptocratic bonuses reflect the impersonal and value-free workings of a rational market in tune only with supply and demand. They do not. They reflect ancient practice dating back to the pharaohs of Egypt where a greed-driven top command determines their own rewards. Now consider a recent case where the top command had little to do with setting their own rewards, but instead were paid salaries set by a higher authority. Does that limit or constrain their performance? Well, consider the performance of the U.S. Army during Desert Storm. General Norman Schwarzkopf won one of the most lopsided victories in military history in just 100 hours of combat with hardly any loses. His salary and benefits, at the end of a 30-year career, was 11 times greater than an 18-year-old recruit just entering basic training. By comparison, our financial geniuses whose incompetence nearly destroyed the global financial structure enjoyed earnings of up to 1,000 times greater than one of their entry-level employees. Or consider the compensation and performance of top management at American auto companies, who have always paid themselves scads more than their counterparts in Japan, only to have the competition run circles around them.

Economic history confirms what the punctuated equilibrium process of evolution tells us, namely that unconstrained competition ends with overexploitation followed by a crash, exactly as we saw in 2007–2008. Yet it is just as true that during the equilibrium phase of the process, it is possible to so overregulate competition that equilibrium can lead to stagnation and ultimately, collapse, as it did in the last years of the USSR from 1989 to 1991. So the question arises: "Just how do we strike a reasonable balance between the two?" Specifically, what must the government do to achieve full employment without inflation? How can we also avoid the alternative dangers of authoritarian stagnation or the chaos and collapse of unconstrained competition? How can we have the freedom to innovate and change without going overboard?

My suggestions are as follows:

1. Reregulate the financial sector along the lines that served us so well between 1934 and 1978. To be sure, some adjustments must be made in light of the new electronic technology and today's interconnected global economy. Still, we need not let that technology mislead us as it surely did after 1980. Suddenly we could do lots of neat stuff with the personal computer and Internet, and we did, and much of it got us into trouble. But, just because you can do it does not mean you should do it. Above all, we need to make sure leverage is sharply constrained. Keep commercial banks and investment banks separate as they were under Glass-Steagall. They have different needs. Maintaining a stable system should trump providing opportunities to get rich quick with new financial innovations or combinations of functions.

2. Eliminate the income tax on corporate partnerships where a large portion (say 85 percent) of the employees are working partners and established legal guidelines for such partnerships are followed, including representation on the board of directors. Partners would pay personal income tax rates as is now the case for most legal partnerships. Eliminating corporate double taxation on corporate partnerships would be an incentive to create real partnerships, not a command to create them. Moreover, unfriendly takeovers of the common stock would have no point if the Board of Directors had enough working partner seats to veto the breaking up of companies and of casting employees aside to "enhance shareholder value" at the expense of the labor force. (How Wall Street financiers would howl if such corporate partnerships could break their overstuffed rice bowls.)

3. Set up constraints on mergers and acquisitions that create companies "too big to fail" in the financial, industrial, and service sectors alike. As it is, the supposed benefits of mergers and acquisitions are routinely overstated, just as the diseconomies of large scale are routinely ignored or understated. The often costly cultural clashes that ensue when different corporate cultures are mashed together similarly get downplayed, though many mergers have suffered or failed because of it. This constraint requires more rigorous enforcement of antitrust laws. In my experience, financial types do not even want this issue discussed, lest it threaten the very big bonuses they anticipate if the merger goes through. And remember, they get their bonus for the deal when it goes through, and they do not have to give it back if the merger or acquisition proves a disaster.

If we regulate and stabilize the financial sector and cease using it as a playpen for get-rich-quick schemes based on high leverage, we will prevent future meltdowns. If we encourage the formation of corporate partnerships that dissolve the adversarial relationship between capital and labor and instead bring them together working for the same goals, we can compete much more effectively with foreign rivals now coming at us from every direction. If we constrain the rush to mergers and acquisitions, many of which prove disastrous anyway, we can avoid getting caught up in the "too big to fail" trap. One of the functions of the free market is that the market impersonally eliminates participants that get too compromised to compete effectively. Yet as we have seen, when a behemoth weakens and fails, there is a real danger that it could wreck the economy in the course of its fall. Moreover, while there are undoubtedly economies of scale as any organization gets larger, beyond a certain point, the diseconomies of scale take over. The finance folks who arrange so many of these mergers typically ignore or lose sight of those diseconomies, just as they do the dangers of a merger between conflicting corporate cultures.

There will of course always be new problems to confront. Many will come unexpectedly, seemingly out of nowhere. If we put our economy on a sound footing, however, we can deal with those surprises much more effectively. This book has tried to point the way to that sound footing.

NOTES

1. Wallace, William McDonald. "The Great Depression Reconsidered; Implications for Today." *Contemporary Economic Policy* 13 (April 1995): 1–15.

2. Behravesh, Nariman. *Spin-Free Economics: A No-Nonsense Guide to Today's Global Economic Debates*. New York: McGraw-Hill, 2009.

3. Ibid., p. 326.

4. Ibid., p. 328.

5. Ibid., p. 329.

6. McCreevy, Charley. *Financial Times*, Feb. 2007 quoted in Behravesh, p. 319.

7. Behravesh, *Spin-five Economics*, p. 321.

8. *Wall Street Journal*, Dec. 15, 2009.

APPENDICES

Several problems not directly contributing to the 2008 market collapse nevertheless need addressing because they affect the political economy on many levels. These are dealt with below. For example the cost of medical care has skyrocketed and become a big and controversial drag on society. It is now about one-sixth of the entire gross domestic product. Unless we can control those costs, we will see increasingly serious problems affecting the political economy. We will address that issue in Appendix A.

In Appendix B we address the issue of globalization as it has evolved by the twenty-first century. Here we deal with the old issue of free trade, long considered a very good policy. Yet times do change. Given today's much different circumstances does free trade still provide a net benefit to our nation? Are we content with seeing our jobs and industries being outsourced abroad? Are we comfortable watching whole factories being sent abroad to produce goods for export back to the United States for consumption? Many a former advocate of free trade has jumped ship on that issue. Obviously the jobs issue affects how we employ labor. Will we continue to employ labor on a contingent basis as a commodity? Some might say free trade favors that policy. Or will we begin to employ labor as permanent partners in the company with a real, long-term interest in its success?

What about the 12 million illegal immigrants that live and work here? We look at this seemingly intractable issue in Appendix C. America seems to have lost control of our own immigration and cannot seem to come up with a satisfactory answer. It is dangerous to pass laws we cannot or will not enforce because it serves certain interests not to enforce them. This issue seems to be caught in a political gridlock of conflicting interests. Still, we propose a possible solution to this problem.

In Appendix D we look at the need to protect our environment without also devastating the economy. Human economies may or may not account for global warming, but given the degree of melting of the ice cap in the Arctic Ocean and of glaciers the world over, who can doubt that global warming is taking place? Moreover, we cannot doubt that huge amounts of both air and water pollution are directly caused by human activity. Meanwhile, ground water levels are falling fast in the Midwest and elsewhere in the world. If they drop much further we will face a huge problem. Finally some of these problems are global in nature and cannot be solved by individual nations working in isolation. That raises some truly troubling questions that feed back into the issue of globalization and the old issue of the whole versus the parts that plays out in all kinds of contexts.

Appendix E considers a truly troubling issue that also feeds back into globalization, namely energy supplies in the context of the terrorism perpetrated by Islamic fundamentalists who are partly financed by the oil money Islamic nations enjoy thanks to insatiable purchasers like us. We will also propose a possible solution here, one that will at least let us better defend ourselves from that terrorism.

APPENDIX A: THE HIGH COST OF MEDICAL CARE VERSUS THE LOW COST OF HEALTH CARE

The cost of medical care has escalated into one of the major costs of the American economy. It is about one-sixth of the gross domestic product. The cost of medical care exceeds the net profits of most major corporations. Yet the debate about this issue is misleadingly labeled as a debate about "health care." That label is simply a semantic trick; they really mean medical care. The trick is to make it seem that politicians are talking about health care when they specifically want to avoid any real discussion of it.

Good health care is about *how to stay healthy.* The way to assure good health is to live a healthy lifestyle. That issue is not being debated; it is deliberately excluded from the discussion. The debate instead concerns medical insurance, its cost, and who should pay for it. The cost of medical insurance and who can afford it is of course a major issue. It is one that must be addressed. But how to stay healthy, and thus reduce the need for medical care, is equally vital, since it is poor health that is driving up the cost of medical care to unsustainable levels. And in too many cases, that poor health comes from so many people choosing to live toxic lifestyles.

For years this issue of medical insurance was debated as such. Do we want socialized medical care or not? How are we going to make sure all who need medical care can get it? If the answer is to offer federal subsidies to the poor—and tax the rich to pay for them—then let us debate that issue, as we did for years. When we implemented the federal program called Medicare in the sixties, for example, we did not call it "Healthcare." Soon after Hillary Clinton's complicated plan of universal medical care collapsed in the early 1990s, we began substituting the term "health care" for "medical care." Among other things, it was clear that the rates of obesity, adult diabetes, drug abuse, and other similar diseases were rising and doing so despite improved medical technology and medicines. The question was: Why?

One major reason is that many people do not take good care of their health. Many people continue to smoke, for instance, despite massive evidence that smoking is a major cause of lung cancer, throat cancer, and emphysema. That fact raises a nasty question. If we are going to talk about socialized medicine or government-subsidized medical insurance, should taxpayers who take good care of their own health have to pay the cost of "self-inflicted wounds" and in effect subsidize a toxic lifestyle?

That is, of course, a divisive political question. It highlights a fault line that divides conservatives and liberals. Liberals focus on compassion and conservatives focus on personal responsibility. In our postwar debates about socialized medicine, both sides more or less took for granted that most people did what they could to maintain personal health. Not even the critics of socialized medicine talked about "self-inflicted wounds." Alcoholism was by then considered a disease, and it was not yet widely believed that cigarettes caused serious health problems except among "puritan prudes" who did not count.

The biggest fraud in the current debate is the claim that millions of people cannot afford good health care so the taxpayers must step in to help the less fortunate. Liberals often make the claim that it is not fair to deny access to affordable health care to umpteen million people. Of course it is not fair. Here, however, is where the fraud comes in. The fact of the matter is that anyone can afford good health care because *generally, a healthy lifestyle costs less, not more*. Quit smoking, for example, and you save about $1,500 per year. Quit drinking and you may save as much or even more depending on how much and how often you drink. Substitute fresh fruit of the season for sweets, and more vegetables for fat and sugar soaked pastries and you will save more yet. All those savings translate into better health and less disease. Walk more and watch TV less and you gain even more health at virtually no cost. Such savings would generate the cash to pay for a lot of medical insurance. The risk of cancer, emphysema, and other diseases would drop sharply; we would see lower rates of diabetes, stroke, heart attacks, and much else.

The government's role in health care meanwhile, enjoys bipartisan support. Everyone agrees things such as public safety via police protection, public sanitation, clean water, safe streets, and air traffic control cannot be done well by market forces. The government has to do it. But if you choose to drink too much, smoke too much, drug too much, eat too much or eat too many toxic junk foods, such choices are your personal right. In some traditions, of course, *it is also your personal responsibility to deal with the medical consequences of your own foolish choices*. That view is now politically incorrect in most current debate about medical costs and care.

When we began to realize the nation was slowly adopting increasingly toxic lifestyles, liberals could not accept the idea that people should take personal responsibility for their health instead of expecting the government to care for sick people. For their part, conservatives resisted the idea that taxpayers should be *forced* to finance liberal compassion, especially for the foolish people who make bad health choices. Ah, but hold on. Many conservatives also saw that to withhold treatment for self-inflicted diseases would be politically unpopular and would probably cost them votes. It would seem too cold-blooded a policy.

Some conservatives even admit it is better for the government to pay rather than the responsible individual. Why? Most families probably feel that they are obligated to pick up much of the tab for loved ones who abuse themselves. They would feel guilty not taking care of good old Uncle Charley who came down with lung cancer because of heavy smoking, despite much nagging to quit. If my uncle has no medical insurance, I should pay for his treatment; but what if I cannot without going bankrupt? On second thought, let's let all the other taxpayers help me pick up the tab.

Thus the switch in terms creatively solved the political dilemma, first by obscuring and then outflanking the issue of personal responsibility for one's own health and medical care. Suddenly "health care" was to be a responsibility of the taxpayer. And conservatives went along, although with "health care" as a replacement term for medical insurance, even if they did not lead the charge.

Still, we are left with a serious moral hazard, because a "compassionate" approach subtly enables and even encourages people to continue leading unhealthy lifestyles. They need only go along with the fiction that the government has taken over "health care" by providing the medical insurance that pays for the medical consequences of leading an unhealthy lifestyle. We cannot escape the fact that having a healthy population is a socially useful goal. It thus is vital that individuals practice a healthy lifestyle. But neither can we escape the fact that actual care of our health care is a matter of individual lifestyle choices. Therefore, given any system of sharing costs of medical care, however labeled, individuals implicitly acquire an obligation to practice a healthy lifestyle. Yet we do not want to seem guilty of trying to enforce that obligation. Meanwhile, the current fiction that government-funded insurance takes care of our health could eventually bankrupt the country if we continue living unhealthy lives that drive up medical care costs.

Here, let us review the philosophical standoff between liberal compassion for the less fortunate, and the conservative's ethic of personal responsibility for our own bad choices. That standoff, again, created a political dilemma that was solved by creating the fiction that subsidized medical insurance amounts to providing "health care." How does this fit in with the FROCA process?

In good part it relates to the explosive post-World War II growth of the processed junk food industry. That industry accounts for a growing part of the nation's bad health, and particularly for obesity and adult diabetes. Junk foods (and fast foods) are very popular and therefore profitable to make and sell. In the impersonal world of supply and demand, if the public demands something, suppliers should be free to supply it. Many of these junk foods taste good, often provide a sense of comfort, and yet frequently seem somewhat addictive. They are also very convenient. Serving heavily sugared cold cereal that your children will eat without complaint beats cooking breakfast when both parents work. Children easily get hooked on junk food. These foods cause health problems when they are consumed in quantity because their good taste is usually the result of high amounts of sugar, fats, and salt that are unhealthful to humans in excessive quantities. They also cause problems when they are eaten instead of real food, because they are very poor in real nutrients. Even when artificial sweeteners replace sugar, health problems can emerge. Moreover, the onset of health problems comes later. The pleasure of eating junk food comes now. Junk foods are often called "comfort foods." Like booze, they convey comfort now, whereas the cirrhosis or weight gain comes later. Almost no one becomes addicted to substances that cause some displeasure right now (cod liver oil?) but can improve health later on.

In short, the junk food industry has created a very large block of dedicated consumers and willing suppliers among both liberals and conservatives. The consumers and suppliers are happy to support the fiction that government supported medical insurance amounts to health care. They are supported by libertarians, those people who feel citizens should be free to consume as they choose as well as to supply consumers anything they demand.

In FROCA terms, the introduction of the large-scale production of processed food loaded with sugar, salt, oil, and such created a new frontier of opportunity. That frontier has been vigorously exploited for the last 50 years. The bad health such food can cause, of course, threatens a crash sooner or later. The industry might avoid such a crash if it can transform itself into a supplier of good, nutritious food that promotes good health. (And already a few companies are pointing in that direction.) But that will not happen on a wide scale unless the demand is there. True enough, a number of self-help groups, such as Alcoholics Anonymous and other similar 12 step programs, have arisen to deal with the various addictions people develop. These are helping. Smoking is down, drinking is down, more people exercise, and all that is to the good. In aggregate, however, all that is not enough. The toxic temptations are just too great. (While writing these words, I finished off a couple of delicious, but oil-saturated and heavily sweetened cookies. Had they been taxed properly, perhaps I would not have bought them.)

The downside is that thousands of jobs in the junk food industry might vanish if people began eating right. So would thousands of jobs in the medical industry if more people were healthy and got sick less. Unfortunately, the livelihood of many workers in the food industry depends on consumers hurting their health by using those products. Better health in turn reduces the number of jobs in the medical care industry. But substituting partners for hirelings as the standard way to employ people would make such adjustments vastly easier.

The solution comes by recognizing the concept of "externalities," a valid insight of neoclassical economics. Now, I have attacked neoclassical economics throughout this book, but the model still contains many things worth preserving, and the concept of externalities is one of them. The production and distribution of almost anything has both internal and external costs. For example the financial, production, and distribution costs of what we consume are internal. The cost of disposing of the waste products is external as are the costs of pollution, and in this case, the medical costs of consuming things that make us sick.

The cost of cigarettes, for example, is more than just the land, labor, and capital that go into producing and distributing them. Additional costs are incurred in treating such diseases as lung cancer and emphysema that are directly caused by using cigarettes. Here is an illustration. A colleague of mine from Boeing contracted lung cancer in his early fifties. He had smoked since he was a teenager, say about 34 years. Do the math and we find he consumed about 12,000 packs of cigarettes or about 240,000 cigarettes. Now, during the last two years before he died, the medical treatment he received (paid by Boeing insurance) cost a total of $440,000. Thus the "external cost" of my colleague's smoking was about $2.00 per cigarette or $40.00 per pack in today's prices. One suspects that had that cost been included in the price of cigarettes, he may well not have taken up smoking. The cost of $40 a pack would have been an enormous disincentive to take up or continue smoking. Had such a tax been in effect, he might have led a healthier life and still be alive.

Thus, one way to cover the cost of providing everyone universal medical care (whether via the government or private insurance) would be to subject all toxic, health-degrading products to taxation at a level comparable to their degree of toxicity and hence external costs. People would remain free to choose to follow an unhealthy lifestyle. But that tax would also ensure that they would be paying their own external costs for their toxic lifestyle. Those who choose a healthy lifestyle would not have to pay the medical costs of those who do not so choose. The cost of comfort foods would go up sharply, I suspect, but the burden for those who indulge only occasionally would be incidental. (When I get writer's block I often lust for one of Denny's mega banana splits, but I only succumb once or twice a month so the cost would be modest.)

In the past when "sin taxes" were discussed on such things as alcohol and tobacco, the critics of such taxes often claimed they were regressive because they hit poor people harder than others. Besides, the critics went on, lots of people do not believe consumption of alcohol or tobacco is a sin. So why tax those items just to please a bunch of blue-nosed prudes? Those products may not be sinful in themselves, to be sure. But, if they are consumed on a large scale, they have proved beyond doubt to contribute to ill health.

What I propose here, however, is not a tax on sin but a tax on toxins that can cause disease and ill health. Those costs must be paid; indeed we are paying for them already—indirectly—as taxpayers. So why not impose a "user's tax"? As for impacting the poor more than others, to the extent the poor are prompted to forsake toxic products (as some now do, of course), they will save far more money, as a percentage of their income, than will the rich. The high costs will fall on those who insist on living a toxic lifestyle. We already have a tax like this on gasoline—those who don't use any gas at all pay nothing; those who use a lot of gas pay a lot.

APPENDIX B: GLOBALIZATION AND FREE TRADE

Since the dawn of civilization, humans have confronted two conflicting tendencies as they battle for control. These tendencies can be defined in various ways: the local versus the global, the periphery versus the center, or the part versus the whole. All the empires of the past fell apart one way or another over some version of this opposition. Conflict between local groups leads to a demand for a strong central government to avoid anarchy and maintain law and order. Border conflicts then lead to a push to create empires, bringing larger regions under uniform control and thereby reducing conflict and increasing safety. The community now also has more or better access to the raw materials needed to sustain the cities that give rise to civilization.

At its peak about 250 CE, Rome had control of all the lands that bordered on the Mediterranean Sea and its various sub-seas. One could safely sail from the Black Sea to the Atlantic Ocean at the Strait of Gibraltar with little risk of piracy. Or one could make the same journey by Roman roads with little risk of being robbed en route. This era was called *Pax Romana*.

Yet, as an empire expands beyond a certain point, keeping central control of local regions becomes increasingly difficult. There will usually be conflict on the border, between the empire and tribes on the other side. The larger the empire, the more extensive its borders and the greater the cost of keeping them under peaceful control. At some point the empire begins to break up as the local tribes in the border regions reassert themselves. The fall of Rome was a classic example. Rome had to expand or else fragment, but a point came when the empire could no longer expand. Rome depended on ever new conquests to finance itself by capturing plunder, slaves, mines, and rich farming lands such as Egypt. But as Rome expanded its border grew more extensive and Rome's powerful legions were spread thinner and thinner. Border tribes grew stronger and better able to attack. It took about 150 years, but Rome finally collapsed as the barbarian hoards began breaking through in the West. Much of the empire fragmented into tribal territories and kingdoms. By 500 CE, the power that was Rome was no more.

In global economics, this same tension between local and global also occurs. Since the end of the Cold War in 1991, a new dynamic has emerged in this conflict, replacing the earlier dynamic of a global economy dominated by two super powers, the USA and USSR, who split control of the world and lived in a tense state of armed truce with each other. The USA promoted a system of universal capitalism and free markets, while the USSR promoted one of universal communism. When the USSR suddenly collapsed in 1991, the Cold War abruptly ended and the present phase of globalization at once began. With the United States standing alone as the world's sole superpower, it seemed at first to usher in the triumph of market capitalism over communist command and control.

But, much else was happening at the same time. Great technological advances had lead to the development of powerful microchips that made possible cheap and powerful personal computers. That in turn soon prompted the creation of a global communications system based on the Internet and World Wide Web. These innovations provided instant and very low-cost communications around the globe. Suddenly, we had an electronic global village for better *and for worse.* The cost constraints of time and distance had suddenly all but vanished. But seen from another perspective, the protection that costly space had long provided different cultures was overcome. It is easy to accept or ignore cultural differences when they are a long way off; and we do not have to live with them. But, when those differences, go counter to your own sacred values, are suddenly thrust right in your face, such up close confrontations can foster intolerance and fragmentation. Close-knit cultural cliques soon form. To avoid conflict, they scarcely interact with each other. In the "cultural clash" between the secular West and Islamic fundamentalism that we are now in, technology has also played a significant role. (See Appendix E) That clash does not preclude commercial interaction, but it does complicate it, and it encourages a "cautious, impersonal approach."

Adam Smith's eighteenth-century theory of free trade held that real increases in wealth come from improved productivity of labor. He went on to show through the example of his famous pin factory that a division of labor can sometimes improve productivity by huge amounts. His third point was that trade barriers such as embargoes or tariffs interfere with the division of labor. They allow or encourage countries to produce inefficiently for themselves some things that other countries could produce more efficiently and cheaply. David Ricardo went further, arguing that a nation should even import things they could produce more cheaply themselves, if importation freed up assets that could be used to get higher returns in other areas with a bigger advantage. My favorite example of this principle, on a personal level, is the hypothetical instance of highly skilled brain surgeon who also happens to be a champion speed-typist capable of 150 words per minute. Assuming that a surgeon is much better paid than a typist, any time spent typing rather than doing surgery in the operating room for this surgeon is a net loss. She would be much better off hiring a typist who could type only 80 words per minute, the typist's wage being but a very small percentage of what the surgeon earns for that same time.

From 1776 to about 1996 nearly all economists supported the Smith/Ricardo theory of free trade. But when all that new electronic technology—a technology that an economist of the eighteenth century could not even imagine—really began to take hold and give rise to our "electronic global village," twenty-first-century economists began to have second thoughts. After all, the new technology was changing the context and the parameters of free trade. Until then it was supposed that high tech nations would cede labor-intensive industries to the less-developed nations. The developed nations would instead concentrate on higher tech industries to replace lost jobs. That pattern worked reasonably well when the new technology was mainly mechanical. It broke down, however, when electronic technology took over.

As the twenty-first century dawned, the United States suddenly appeared vulnerable to losing not only labor-intensive industry, but high-tech stuff as well. Out of almost nowhere, India seemed to leap into action to take over the high-tech call-center business. (Why India rather than others? Because so many Indians spoke good English and had technical educations.) The Indians were paid as little as 25 percent of their American equivalents. With personal computers increasingly interconnected via the World Wide Web, it often turned out much cheaper to export high-tech design work as well. Not only that, but electronics all but revolutionized supply-chain management, with Walmart leading the way. Huge cost savings were possible by shifting from American to Chinese suppliers for almost any manufactured product, now that you could keep electronic track of everything the whole time. Besides that, China could adopt the high-tech labor-saving manufacturing techniques as easily as could American companies and still pay less than a third the wages. Finally, more and more companies began to export whole factories, along with their jobs. They then staffed those jobs in the exported factories with low-cost local labor and re-exported the factory's output back to America for consumption.

Whoa, hold on, many economists began to say. We did not sign up for this sort of thing. Maybe the bottom line is not the only thing that counts in life. Maybe a sense of community cohesion should trump a purely free-market reallocation of resources.

Global interdependence is all well and good . . . but only up to a point. The world has many cultures with sharply differing values. Those differences put serious constraints on socioeconomic integration. Maybe the time will come when diverse cultures spontaneously integrate from the bottom up into one giant melting pot. But the facts of history and the process of evolution so far suggest otherwise. The long-term trend of evolutions suggests that fragmentation will continue. Even religions and secular ideologies have not seriously reversed this trend. Consider the two major secular ideologies, namely capitalism and communism. Both ideologies proclaimed universal solutions to socio-politico-economies based on industrial technology. Both saw the development of factions almost from the outset. Capitalism, it is true, allows for cultural diversity. For some time free-market enthusiasts claimed free-market capitalism really worked only under constitutional democracies. But the early rise of an authoritarian Japan and the more recent rise of a neo-communist China raised big questions about that premise. Moreover, Hitler, Mussolini, and Franco all kept markets intact, but tried to regulate and closely control them in various ways.

Indeed, China's unique blend of market capitalism and neo-communism has given China a gigantic comparative advantage over the United States. The United States has passed many laws and imposed many regulations when it comes to construction, public or private. Many different agencies must approve the permits. Required environmental impact statements must be written and are subject to multiple levels of review and approval. Often the law of eminent domain must be invoked so the government can take over the land. That land or other property must be paid for at market prices. The market price can lead to serious disputes if the market is thin. Construction projects can be challenged in the courts by almost anyone for almost anything. We bend over backward to let everyone have a voice. But all that takes significant time and money.

Such governance has become a general problem in America. Bill Lockyer, the state treasurer of California, who has held office for 35 years, has said, "We're part of a system that is designed not to work" (*Palm Springs [Calif.] Desert Sun*, 10/26/09). He goes on to say that our system of checks and balances, designed to avoid the problems of a distant central authority running the country, worked fairly well at first. The country had a more or less unified culture at the time the Constitution was written. But even then the new republic had problems when the two value systems regarding slavery could not be resolved by negotiations. It was finally resolved by the bloodiest war in our history between the North and the South.

Today our economy, thanks to our democratic system, drags a huge anchor. We have created so many hurdles to jump over and hoops to jump through before a decision can be finalized on almost any construction. We are operating with a system designed to fit the situation of the eighteenth century. And until we redesign the system to accommodate the twenty-first century cultural reality, according to Lockyer, we will have more and more political gridlock: "You are the captive of this environment and I don't see any way out."

One indication of this problem is that the California Legislature, one long-controlled by liberal Democrats in a very liberal state, has a 13 percent approval rating in the polls. Similarly, the approval rating for the current Democratic U.S. Congress as of this writing (October 2009) is barely 21 percent.

The Chinese government can skip all these hurdles and hoops we impose on ourselves because it owns all the land in China. It simply stamps the word "approved" on a project and it moves right ahead. Thus, the Chinese can get a new project up and running long before we Americans can even get all the permits approved. That fact of course gives many companies a strong incentive to locate new projects abroad, together with the low-cost employment they provide. Consequently, China has now achieved the highest rate of sustained economic growth ever, even greater than Japan's earlier record 1947–1990. China's economic advantage, of course, reflects the fact that they do not impose a tax to recoup the external costs on what they produce. Their seriously eroded environment reflects the same fact. Indeed, China could experience a major environmental crash at almost any time because of the great air and water pollution it has produced since transforming itself into a quasi-market economy. Our environment is much cleaner as a result of our hoops and hurdles, but the cost to us in competitive disadvantage and slowed growth is great and getting worse.

The idea that electronic technology created a global economy to everyone's advantage is now dead. The global collapse in 2008 could not have happened without our electronic technology. It was that technology that enabled us to move billions and even trillions of dollars around overnight. Technology createth wealth to be sure, but it is equally true that technology sometimes taketh away wealth, too, and often in a flash. Just how we will adjust to the new reality of high-tech crosscurrents and multiple points of view, of clashing values stoutly defended, that remains to be seen. What is certain is that the idea of free trade always and everywhere being the best answer for everyone is dead. We very much need to adjust our economic theories accordingly. But let me predict one likely subject for a lively twenty-first century debate. Resolved: Market fascism has a comparative economic advantage over market democracy. Up to now, market democracy has had, and seems to continue to have, a big advantage when it comes to the freedom to innovate. Will a liberal fascist approach trump that advantage by developing our innovations coming from our freedoms faster and more effectively than we can?

Early in the history of American industry, we got most of our innovations from Europe, but we developed them much faster than Europe. Europe's innovators then began coming to America in droves. In recent decades America has done most of the innovating but the Asians seem quicker about getting our innovations to market. Certainly that has been true of consumer electronics. But will our freedom to innovate continue to attract innovators to come here, given the constraints that now encumber development? Or will Asia be the land of opportunity for twenty-first century entrepreneurs? These are all vital questions for the future of globalization, and they all involve nasty questions of priorities and tradeoffs.

The general tension between the whole and the part deeply divides liberals from conservatives. Broadly speaking, conservatives see themselves speaking and acting on behalf of the United States; they extol the virtues of patriotism and want to "put America first." Conservatives promote free trade to be sure, but on the premise that free trade helps the United States. Conservatives say the world is better off with free trade, but the dirty little secret about free trade remains true: No nation ever climbed to the top of the heap by practicing free trade. Britain developed a passion for free trade only *after* they became "the world's workshop" and foremost industrial power. The United States was a protectionist nation right up to the end of World War II at which time, with

6 percent of the world's population, we produced 50 percent of the world's goods and services. Our main motive for free trade—along with acquiring favorable markets for our goods—was to acquire allies against the Soviet Union. Britain's motive earlier was the same: to keep the United States friendly in the event Britain came in conflict with the continental powers of Europe. Farsighted those Brits, and so were we in keeping Germany and Japan on our side for the last 50 years.

Liberals have long had a reputation of devaluing patriotism, which they often dismiss as provincialism. Liberals have a more cosmopolitan view of the world, and they strongly promote cultural diversity if not the diversity of ideas. They are also distinctly more aligned with urban culture and values while conservatives tend to be better represented in the regions lying beyond the big cities. (If one views the 2004 elections as red and blue counties instead of whole states, the difference is immediately apparent. Urban counties voted for Kerry and were overwhelmingly liberal, rural counties voted for Bush and were overwhelmingly conservative.)

While America was the sole superpower, the liberal's cosmopolitan point of view served a useful purpose. But our relative status is in rapid decline, and that decline is likely to shift the prevailing focus from the interests of the whole world—where we can no longer presume ourselves the top dog—to a more specific concern for the United States' own vital interests, now increasingly seen as in conflict with powerful competitive forces. Another way to put it is to quote the old bromide: All politics is local politics.

APPENDIX C: IMMIGRATION REFORM

The commodity theory of labor has played a part in allowing more than 12 million illegal immigrants to come into the United States. Most of them hold various kinds of jobs, but there are a fair number of felons and career criminals as well. The situation is highly controversial, of course. Some liberals want to offer blanket amnesty to the illegals. "Ask and citizenship shall be given." Moreover, many liberals would erect no barriers to further free immigration. Liberals taking such a position are usually accused of hoping that the illegals, of whatever nationality, would out of gratitude for liberal-sponsored free citizenship, become loyal Democrats. Meanwhile, the liberal governments of a number of municipalities have made them "Sanctuary Cities" affording the illegals some protection from being found out and deported. They do that by prohibiting the police from checking for citizenship even if arrested for major felonies. Those with long rap sheets, who are clearly career criminals, sometimes get such protection. Many of those so protected have gone out to rape and murder again.

On the other extreme, some conservatives want the illegals deported with no further ado: They broke the law; get rid of them. The vast majority of people, I suspect reject both of those extremes. There are all sorts of quite different interests at work here, including the desire to import cheap labor as a commodity for work in the fields. Many farmers insist native-born Americans simply refuse to work on farms as manual labor. Meanwhile certain businesses, especially those engaged in landscaping, the hotel and tourist industry, maintenance, construction, and some light manufacturing depend heavily on the labor of the illegal immigrants, few of whom even speak basic English. I now live in the Palm Springs, California, area, and many communities here in the Coachella Valley probably could not function without the labor of these undocumented workers. Even if mass deportation were possible, which it most clearly is not, it would prove catastrophic for many communities.

Still, something has to be done. The current situation creates all sorts of problems. Many previously well-established English speaking communities have been virtually pushed out of existence by the mass intrusion of illegal immigrants, and who also benefit from a full suite of civil rights protection. While ethnic disruption and transformation of neighborhoods have long taken place with the successive waves of earlier, mostly legal immigrants, the process was usually more gradual. Many native-born Americans today complain that upon returning to their hometowns later as adults, they felt like they had entered a third world country where they did not even know the language.

Aside from the displacement problem, taxpayers are forced to pay for schooling, extra police protection, and medical care they cannot afford on current tax revenues. Some border area hospitals have been forced to shut down because they have gone broke treating illegal immigrants for free in emergency rooms (as federal law mandates they must). Undocumented workers do pay sales taxes, and when employed on the books, also have payroll taxes deducted from their pay. Still, many work off the books to keep a low profile, and thus pay no income or Social Security taxes. Meanwhile, much of the income illegal workers earn is exported back to family members in their home countries. As much as $20 billion a year is being thus exported, significantly contributing to America's massive balance of payments deficit.

If people can come into the United States illegally, speaking no English, and then continue to live in closed communities speaking only their native language, and take jobs in situations where they are able to speak only their native language, without being required to learn English, they will be slow to integrate into American culture. There is a left-wing school of thought that supports such cultural fragmentation. For some decades now such groups have insisted that the old idea of the melting pot was a bad thing. They want the melting pot metaphor replaced by the metaphor of the salad bowl. The idea is that each culture that comes into America has a right to survive without being "contaminated" by America's Anglo Saxon and "racist" cultural founders. Such groups go on to argue that it is racist to claim one culture is superior to another. All cultures, languages, and cultural values in this view have a right and deserve to be regarded and treated as equals. There is logic to that statement purely in the abstract.

But that is a trivial truth because in the real world of evolution, fitness is never an abstraction. Fitness is always specific to the environment and its ecology. What is fit in one context can be hopeless in another. We can again refer to Jared Diamond to illustrate. Diamond points out that the hunter-gatherer cultures of Papua in Eastern New Guinea, which he has long studied, would be hopelessly unfit if plopped into the middle of urban Los Angeles where Diamond teaches. He then goes on to point out that the reverse is also equally true: He, Jared Diamond, if plopped in the middle of a Papuan jungle on his own would be just as hopelessly unfit. In other words cultures always evolve to fit the specific features of their environment.

The specifics of our earth's environments differ sharply on many different levels. It is absurd to say they are equal unless all are detached from any environment of any kind. In that case, the argument for equality is both meaningless and misleading. That the "all cultures are equal" argument could even be made shows just how completely the social sciences remain innocent of the evidence of evolution and therefore, just how easy it is for them to deduce a false reality from the dogma of their ideology.

Lest I be accused of an anti-liberal bias here, let me assure the reader that the conservatives do exactly the same thing. In a similar vacuum devoid of evidence from evolution, conservatives also deduce a false reality from their ideology. That fact gives rise to much unrealism in the neoclassical model's view of ever-rational investors. They supposedly never become irrationally exuberant in lusting to "get rich quick" when leverage is at hand.

The bottom line, however, is that the "melting pot" metaphor is a much more realistic metaphor for a healthy American culture. Policies that would instead try to preserve the "salad bowl" simply invite Balkanization, a term that implies institutionalized and debilitating internal conflict. Yet some liberals would even defend that result, because they fantasize themselves acting as referees to insure such conflicts always have "politically correct" outcomes, and that in turn implies a fascist state. In the real world of wide genetic variations in people and even wider technological variations in culture, the only way to cancel the natural variations in fitness and thus assure equality in outcomes is an authoritarian government that can coercively enforce that policy. If, on the other hand, we have a government that enforces a policy of equality of opportunity, different degrees of fitness guarantee a wide variation in outcomes.

So, what should be done about illegal immigrants? What policies can we devise that can bring them into the American mainstream? In my view we need a program that offers to all except dangerous felons a real chance to earn the right to naturalized citizenship. At the outset of such an offer, we must end the practice of sanctuary cities. We must promptly deport those who commit felonies and cannot prove citizenship or other legal status.

If that stricture is imposed at the same time that we create a clear path for current illegal immigrants to become naturalized citizens, it would not hurt law-abiding people. By applying for citizenship, illegal immigrants could at once acquire the provisional status of a legal resident and be given a card to that effect. The path to citizenship would involve four stages. (1) Candidacy would be granted when a person applies and submits fingerprint, hair, and DNA samples for identification. (2) The candidate must agree to have Social Security deductions surcharged by say an additional 5 percent of gross income, or about 12 percent in total until all the requirements for citizenship are completed. As an incentive to complete the process, including learning basic English, 25 percent of that surcharge would be refunded to the newly certified citizen. (3) The candidate must satisfy the existing qualification requirements applicable to all applicants for citizenship. (4) Finally, the candidate must demonstrate satisfactory competence in speaking, understanding, and writing basic English. People identified as illegal immigrants who choose not to apply for citizenship could be given a one-way airplane ticket back to their own country.

This plan would have a good chance of speeding up the integration of the present illegal population into American culture. Those who reject American culture for whatever reason are free to leave and go to whatever culture better fits their preferences.

But what about the problem of a continuing in-flow of illegals? Almost nothing America has done, including several amnesty programs, has stopped their arrival. The 2008 meltdown helped stem the flow and to some extent even reversed it as jobs dried up. A surcharge on Social Security deductions for all employed illegal immigrants would possibly discourage some from coming into the country to work illegally. Eliminating sanctuary cities and empowering police to check on the status of those suspected of being illegals would inhibit some illegal immigration. Collecting fingerprints, hair, and DNA samples of any caught trying to pass the border illegally would inhibit even more.

APPENDIX D: THE ECONOMY AND THE ENVIRONMENT

Given the massive loss of ice from the polar ice cap and the mountain glaciers around the world, there can be little doubt that global warming is actually taking place. Otherwise, why did all that ice melt, and so quickly, much of it in just the past 50 years? Nevertheless, two questions arise about which reasonable people might differ. First, to what extent does human activity account for the warming? Some argue that humans cause a good deal of that warming. Others argue it is mostly just another cycle of climatic swings that the earth has experienced for at least a half billion years. Moreover, several ice ages have come and gone while the human population was too tiny to matter. So why blame ourselves for this latest cycle? I believed that school of thought until about 2002.

What changed my mind? The research on my book, *Techno-Cultural Evolution*, allowed me to make an estimate of the impact of human activity on the environment since humans began farming about 10,000 years ago. Global population at that time is usually estimated at about 6 million people. Today, the number is approaching 7 billion, over 1,000 times more people. Then too, 10,000 years ago we were mainly nomadic hunter-gatherers. We left a very light footprint with that lifestyle, even though we often set brush fires to drive game animals over cliffs or into bogs and marshes where they were trapped. If we give that lifestyle an index value 1.0, we can make reasonable estimates of how our footprint has increased. In today's industrial world, with our huge infrastructure investments in cities, transportation, dams, canals, mines, industrial plants, and just plain consumption, I made a very crude estimate that the human average footprint index per capita would be 100. Multiply that value by the factor of 1,000 to account for population increase, then total footprint rose by about 100,000 fold. Now that increase spread out over 10,000 years does not represent a particularly alarming rate of change per year or even per century. To me the frightening statistic was this: Of the 100,000-fold estimated increase over 10,000 years, fully 50 percent of it came since I left college in 1952. That is, the population tripled and per capita consumption has skyrocketed. From one motor vehicle per family in the United States in 1950, the ratio is now closer to one vehicle per person. Huge areas of the world that essentially had no motor vehicles to speak of in 1950, China, Japan, and India for example, are now awash in them. Smog is dense in the once clear skies of China today, from one end of the nation to the other.

In short, the sudden sharp increase in the melting of ice caps and glaciers correlates almost precisely with the sharp increase in the human footprint. But hold on, the skeptic might say, even with that sharp increase in human consumption, the vast amount of CO_2 in the atmosphere even now comes from such natural causes as the rotting of biomass. Human consumption accounts for only four to five percent. Yet, our share is up from one or two percent. That is a very big and very quick relative change. Still, the total does not seem alarming, that is until one introduces the reality of chaos theory. Chaos theory tells us that even small changes in initial conditions, can, via positive feedback loops, progressively accelerate into a very large change in later outcomes. With respect to melting ice caps, we can indeed see a very clear positive feedback loop.

It works as follows: Ice reflects about 90 percent of the sunlight's heat back into space. Blue water, however, absorbs about 90 percent of sunlight's heat and thus begins to warm the water. The warmer water for its part will speed up the melting of ice, thus increasing the area of blue water. The blue water thus begins to absorb even more heat, just as the declining area of the ice pack reflects less heat, and so on. This clearly is positive feedback. If left to itself, the ice will melt at increasing rates and force up average global temperatures. It is also clear a relatively small change in global warming could trigger such a loop.

The ice/water ratio with respect to sunlight is not the only positive feedback loop so far identified. CO_2 is only one greenhouse gas that promotes global warming. A far more potent gas is methane. Methane has about 20 times more global warming power compared to CO_2. Immense amounts of frozen methane are embedded in the permafrost of Siberia, Scandinavia, Canada, and Alaska. That permafrost is itself beginning to melt, and thus beginning to release methane gas. Today, for example, permafrost can support large trucks on Alaska's North Slope only about half as long as in the past few decades. Paleontologists believe that in eons past a sudden great explosion of such melting methane triggered a near extinction event catastrophe. In the present situation, it is clear that these two feedback loops tend to self-accelerate unless something stops them. In any event, those loops pose a potentially serious crisis of an unknown probability. Indeed, a serious environmental crisis could erupt far more quickly than merely linear forecasts (those that ignore nonlinear feedback loops) would suggest.

I am not a climatologist and so I take no dogmatic stand on this issue. But I do know that in climatology and in economics, "computer forecasts" have failed us time and again when they assume a mechanistic or deterministic environment. Those models are often wrong whether predicting more heating or more cooling. Concern over global warming seems to have peaked with the release of Al Gore's movie, *An Inconvenient Truth*, but concern has since cooled down because the weather did too. But unless the glaciers and polar ice caps start expanding again, my hunch is that global warming will continue. Every long-term trend has short periods of reversal.

But is a hunch good enough to go on a crash program of environmental protection? It depends. Much depends on whether the program helps, hurts, or has a neutral economic impact. Environmentalists for years have forced developers to write "environmental impact statements" as a condition of project approval. Conservatives and even moderates are now turning the tables. They demand "economic impact statements" before supporting major environmental protection or "green" projects. Much of the resistance to environmental protection comes from fear that such programs can wreck the economy. And the cruel fact is that, because our economy operates more or less on the assumptions of neoclassical economics, environmental protection projects could indeed heavily damage the economy by wiping out a critical mass of jobs.

Here we come to my bottom line. The reforms suggested in Chapter 11 and Appendices A, B, and C would go far to minimize the damage of many proposed protections. If human activity contributes to global warming, then the blame lies heavily on the vast increase in human consumption, especially since the end of World War II. Our sharp increase in "material standards of living," whatever their effect on global warming, has clearly come at the cost of vast increases in air pollution and the pollution of oceans, rivers, and lakes. This huge surge in spending and consumption has come first because innovative technology developed a host of new products that stimulated demand. The production of these new products helped generate the income to buy them, of course, but beyond that consumers bought way beyond their means with a huge explosion of spending on credit. About 40 percent of the jobs in this country are devoted to supplying this growth of consumption. If consumption holds steady and merely stops growing, most of the jobs servicing the growth will disappear. That is why politicians left, right, and center support economic growth.

Consumers are now being forced to spend less as unemployment rises. In addition, they must spend even less to pay off debt that was once supported by asset values that have now vanished. Those reductions in spending cost jobs in the land of the hirelings, and when jobs go, unemployment rises.

Now add another hit to consumption to reduce air and water pollution and to halt global warming and the country enters a world of hurt. That hurt is amplified if the United States is forced to cut jobs to reduce pollution, global warming, etc. while, say, China and India keep sending us lower cost production. Voters vote their pocketbooks more than they do environmental protection. Politicians respond to that fact. The United States refused to sign the Kyoto agreements on the environment precisely because China and India were exempted. Both Democrats and Republicans rejected Kyoto for that reason.

If, say, 75 percent of our regular labor force worked in partnership with the stockholders, the unit cost of both equity capital and equity labor would be flexible. That cost flexibility would greatly increase a firm's ability to respond to competitive threats. It would also enable a firm and the economy to adjust to environmental constraints. Again, let us be clear why. Given flexible unit labor costs, a downturn means everyone takes some reduction in earnings. But given the rigid unit labor costs of hirelings, the same downturn means lost jobs and people on the street. True, they may collect unemployment compensation, but that does not pay all the bills, never mind compensate for the loss of social status and often a sense of psychological humiliation. Even so, it does put a burden on taxpayers that need not exist, if everyone just received some small reduction in earnings while remaining employed. If partnership between capital and labor became the standard way of using regular labor, in short, the economy as a whole would be strengthened.

APPENDIX E: ENERGY INDEPENDENCE AND ISLAMIC TERRORISM

America's need for energy independence results mainly from terrorism, but not just any terrorism. The terrorism that really matters comes mostly from Islamic fundamentalism. Part of our national problem is that it has become politically incorrect to face up to that fact. In fact, the terrorist label itself is used mainly to obscure the role Islamic fundamentalism plays. George W. Bush himself implemented that policy shortly after 9/11. But if it were not for Islamic fundamentalism, we would not be in Iraq or Afghanistan. We might still count Iran as an ally. Major Hasan would not have gone on his shooting jihad at Fort Hood. We could still admire the twin towers of the World Trade Center.

Even our involvement with Israel would be quite different. The Arabs might not be happy with Israel's presence as an independent nation in Palestine. Yet, except for

Islamic fundamentalism, the other Arab states would likely have accepted Israel in 1948 or 1949. Had they done so, Israel would be about half its present size. But the refusal of Islamic fundamentalists to accept Israel's existence prompted Arab attacks to wipe out Israel in 1956 and 1967 that failed miserably, leaving Israel occupying all the territory between the Mediterranean and the Jordan River north of Egypt and south of Lebanon. But for Islamic intransigence, the United States would never have become such a close ally to Israel.

Much of the international climate since World War II, and most of it in the post-Cold War period, stems directly from fundamentalists who control the theology of Islam. They have made what could have been a reasonably peaceful religion into a force for world terror. Islamic nations happen to sit on a huge proportion of the world's oil reserves. Revenues from that oil finance a fundamentalist jihad of terrorism and violence aimed at extending Islam throughout the whole world. We can hardly separate the issue of oil from that of the Islamic fundamentalists. We would not need to worry about being oil independent if we could purchase oil on the world market at market prices from people who did not believe the United States was the world's Great Satan. America's whole way of life and its secular form of government are viewed by Islamic fundamentalists as abominations in the eyes of God. We are the Great Satan because we defy God's Laws. Who are we infidels to presume to legislate man-made laws, when Allah has already laid out His sacred law, the Sharia, in the Holy Koran?

But it is not only mullahs at work here. Much of the mullahs' power to condemn the United States and its values rests on the fact that many of our values clash directly with values and behavioral standards of Islam that enjoy wide grassroots support among Muslims. The sexual license projected by American movies and TV disgusts many. Our commitment to equality for women may enjoy some support, but remarkably few Muslim women seem concerned. Many Muslim women feel safer enshrouded in their veils and robes because they almost never have to fight off womanizing men. George W. Bush insisted that all people want freedom and admire us for ours. All people do probably want freedom. But many in Asia and the Middle East understand freedom differently than we do. To us, personal freedom is a virtue, but others see it as a selfish license that threatens their own values of social obligation to the group. To people in other cultures, our celebration of individualism is synonymous with promoting personal selfishness. What Muslims see as freedom is freedom from control by foreigners, a freedom that lets them follow their own traditions and values. Those values include great respect for God's authority over human beings, which in practice allows for such things as honor killings, the beating of women who go out without a male relative as an escort, and the right to assassinate those who demean Islam. We see such values as abominations and we want to stamp them out, much as they want to stamp out our values. Indeed Muslim immigrants into Euro-American nations are demanding ever more stridently to be judged by their own law of Sharia, not our civil law.

I mentioned in the section on uniformitarianism that this cultural clash is an example of the clash between the imperatives of punctuation (the West) and the imperatives of equilibrium (the Islamic world). Islam's vision of a brotherhood of all mankind under the single religion of Islam and ruled by Allah's law of Sharia amounts to an effort to establish a permanent state of equilibrium over the globe. The mullahs are telling us that they plan to do away with the messy punctuation phase. For our part, we are fighting to preserve the punctuation phase and those frontiers of change and innovation that go with it. Innovation is a key issue here. Cultural change, in the end, comes from innovation in technology and its "software." A permanent state of equilibrium would quash such innovation much as it was quashed in ancient civilizations before the fall of Rome.

In short, Islamic fundamentalists feel strongly that the power and influence of the United States must be stopped because it stands in the way of bringing the whole world under God's Laws. To reach that goal we all must surrender to Islam. Again let us emphasize: Islamic fundamentalism's clear and oft repeated goal is to bring the entire world together as a single brotherhood under Islam. This brotherhood is *not* to be ruled by democratic processes but by Allah's Law, the Sharia, as spelled out in the Holy Koran. This brotherhood is not to be corrupted by nation states and their parochial interests and feuds. Jihad is to bring about this divinely ordered state of affairs. Mohammed reemphasized that goal on his deathbed and stressed that it takes violence to achieve that goal. That is Allah's supreme will according to the fundamentalist understanding.

Hamas's recently stated goal, for example, goes well beyond the obliteration of Israel. Their slogan is: "Allah is the goal, the Prophet is the model, the Koran is the Constitution, Jihad is its path, *and death in the cause of Allah is its most sublime belief.*"[1] Given today's passion for "vision statements" this one by Hamas is as good as it gets. It is crystal clear, and it has much power. It is highly idealistic in promoting one grand brotherhood of mankind. That is an image that has long had appeal for others including Christians before Islam and Marxists of our own day. The idea of abolishing the nation-state together with such impediments as passports, visas, and work permits is pleasant to ponder. So is the vision where all humanity shares the same laws and values without tribal or ideological or regional disputes. How nice that all sounds, as an ideal.

But some people—and not necessarily only the most downtrodden or injured victims of social injustice—are clearly willing to die in the service of this vision. The pilots of the jets that flew into the World Trade Center towers and into the Pentagon on September 11, 2001, were all middle-class adults. Young boys and even girls from the lower levels of Islamic society volunteer to become body bombers to prove their willingness to die for that vision nearly every day. Never mind that a few of them were pressured or shamed into volunteering. Pressure was also applied to some of Japan's kamikaze pilots, but the great majority became kamikazes out of love of Japan. The same is true of Muslim body bombers.

The sincerity of Muslim true believers willing to die for their cause is a very potent reason for their success. It compares to the early Christians who went with high esprit into Rome's coliseum to be torn apart by lions. Most historians give credit for the successful spread of Christianity in its first couple of hundred years to the willingness of those early martyrs to die bravely for their faith, convinced they would pass on to heaven. Today's young Muslim men can see death in the service of their cause as a true opportunity. They have been told they will gain automatic access to 70-odd celestial nubile virgins for their exclusive pleasure as their reward. It is easy for Westerners to snicker at this vision. But if you are a young Muslim male subjected to rushes of testosterone, one with few prospects of marriage, and you have been told since infancy of this reward of celestial virgins, and you want to believe it, and ultimately you do believe it, you are presented with a goal well worth dying for.

I mention all this to suggest the word "terrorist" obscures much more than it reveals, namely the deeply held fundamentalist beliefs that ground their actions. Most Muslim believers, it is true, are convinced that Allah revealed the Holy Koran to Mohammed via the angel Gabriel in Arabian caves starting in 610 CE. They devoutly believe it is sacrilegious to question this truth since it was divinely revealed. They dare not doubt or make fun of it. They have succeeded in intimidating the West to respect their view. Look at the abject apologies many politically correct Westerners took after the Danish cartoons caused riots throughout the Middle East. *The New York Times* even refused to show the cartoons for fear of being accused of disrespect. Or consider the movie *2012*. After an extended discussion, the producers decided to exempt Islamic holy places from the mass destruction they depict for Christian and other religious holy places. The story is that they were driven not so much by any respect for Islam, but rather by fear that the mullahs would put contracts out on the show's producers. They feared no such thing from the Christians.

Still, probably no more than 20 percent of the world's billion plus Muslims are true believers, or fundamentalists. I suspect well over half have never read the Koran. I suspect that many are atheistic or agnostic and that more than half of all Muslims routinely violate many Islamic precepts against drinking alcohol, eating pork, or womanizing. But especially in the Middle East, "nominal" Muslims do well to keep a low profile and keep skeptical or agnostic thoughts to themselves. They may, in fact, love dogs, but in the Middle East dare not keep one as a pet. In the West, those of us who want truly unconditional love are urged to get a dog. In Islam, the mullahs shun dogs as creatures unclean, on a par with infidels and human excrement. All are abominations in Allah's eyes, and good Muslims will shun them all.

All those nominal believers, however, do not count for two reasons. First, nominal believers have no voice in what is regarded as "theologically correct" in Islam. Control rests with fundamentalist mullahs who are true believers. It is they who lay down the rules of what can even be discussed. Second, true believers easily intimidate nominal believers, and like the Catholic clergy in the Middle Ages, mullahs have the power to punish those who question Islamic doctrine. Moreover, a major reformation has never arisen within Islam, as has been the case with Christianity. In Islam no secular historical discussion of what is real and what is myth is permitted. Islam was never corrupted by the competing values of secular science. These sorts of intellectual discussions were stopped soon after they began 1,000 years ago. While Islam divided into the Sunni and Shiite branches early on, there has never been anything like a Protestant Reformation. Nor again has secular government ever been theologically accepted by Islam as it has been in Christian lands. True, after the Ottoman Empire collapsed at the end of World War I, a secular government was created in Turkey by Kemal Ataturk. And later, after World War II, Nasser created a secular government in Egypt and the Baathist Party created secular governments in Syria and Iraq. However, the fundamentalist mullahs have now come to reject all secular governments as futile efforts to copy the West, and right in the face of Allah's sacred plan.

We badly mislead ourselves by a politically correct denial of all the above, dismissing terrorism as the aberrant acts of insane criminals. These Muslims are not terrorists in their own eyes. They are simply doing God's work with the ultimate goal of bringing about true world peace and the brotherhood of all mankind by means of jihad, the very path God himself commanded and by the violent means God himself authorized. Christians merely sing Christmas carols about such goals; unlike Islam Christianity does not seem intent on taking any practical steps to reach that noble goal. Never mind such a goal can never be reached, not, at least, by humans with our current DNA and the normal process of evolution. There is always a push to create such a world; it has been the drive behind all empires. But the bigger the empire gets the greater the drive to reassert local control, an age-old clash between the part and the whole.

Still that universal goal has much power to energize and empower people who need something certain and solid to cling to in a chaotic world. What could be more certain than revealed truth, widely accepted? When people "get it," they are often willing to die for that divine cause, as we see in the war reports nearly every day. One of the dirty little secrets during our war on terrorism is that, by some estimates, more Christians have converted to Islam than have Muslims to Christianity. Christianity seems highly confused and theologically divided, with the mainline churches driven primarily by a vapid political correctness. Only the fundamentalist Christian churches seem to have much drawing power. That is because they, too, present a clear vision and a set of revealed truths that the confused and weary can cling to and shut out all the confused argument and debate.

People are also willing to die for secular ideologies, such as Nazism and Communism, but now these are morally and intellectually bankrupt. In their heyday, though, the dead certainty proclaimed by Hitler had the power to mesmerize the German people. Marx did not claim revealed truth; rather he proclaimed an equally certain scientific determinism that he called historical determinism, which he believed could not be stopped. The German population long remained mesmerized by Hitler, despite the terror of round-the-clock Allied bombing and despite the enormous number of their soldiers killed in battle. The population did not break until the bitter end when on land, at sea, and in the air, the Allied juggernaut had obliterated Germany's military power. The same was true of Japan, but it took the atomic bomb to break the Japanese.

Osama bin Laden was not joking when he said his terror against the United States would end only when we converted to Islam and adopted the Sharia. He offers us the same terms of unconditional surrender we offered the three Axis powers in World War II. We simply dismiss bin Laden as a fanatic and a probable nut. We refuse to understand where Islamic fundamentalists such as bin Laden are coming from. We ignore or dismiss the sincerity of Islamic views. We claim they are corruptions foisted on the population by madmen mullahs. Those views, however, are not corruptions of an earlier peaceful theology. From 620 to 1683, when the Ottomans were repulsed at the gates of Vienna, Islam was on the warpath. Islam's mythical peaceful era never happened. Jihad is a core concept in Islamic theology that Mohammed first gave voice to about 620 CE. The more peaceful parts of the Koran came before Mohammed made his Hegira from Mecca to Medina. After that time, he shifted roles; from a peaceful prophet in Mecca, he became a warrior chief in Medina who set out to conquer Arabia and did so, surprisingly quickly. His successors took up the cause and drove all the way to Tours, France in the west and to the Indus River in the east, in just over 100 years.

As warrior chief, Mohammed's religious "revelations" suddenly began justifying slaughter and mayhem. These passages often contradicted earlier more peaceful revelations. Where passages in the Koran contradict each other, the post-Medina passages trump the earlier Mecca passages. On average, therefore, violence tends to trump peace and mercy in the Holy Koran. Now, one could certainly call this shift in tone and emphasis from prophet to warrior a corruption. But try selling that notion to the Muslims and you risk the mullahs taking out a contract for your execution, as they did on Salman Rushdie. Mohammed founded Islam, not as just another monotheistic religion, but as a thoroughgoing political theocracy that aims to capture the world in its vision by the violent overthrow of the existing order if necessary. Today's mullahs have not corrupted this early Islamic vision of peace and brotherhood through violence and terror. They are making an all-out effort to revive it after a lapse of several hundred years into Islamic Imperialism. Efraim Karsh's whole book, cited earlier, clearly documents that point.

Consider the initial and politically correct reactions to Major Nidal Malik Hasan's massacre of 13 Fort Hood soldiers. The politically correct media bent over backwards to avoid facing the obvious truth. They wanted to see Hasan as psychologically disturbed. They wanted to see him as the victim of harassment. (Someone tore a pro-Islam bumper sticker off his car.) Yet, when Hasan shouted the universal Islamic Jihad slogan, *Allahu Akbar*, he clearly wanted us to see that in his own mind he was indeed doing Allah's work. After shouting his slogan Major Hasan fired off over 100 rounds into a dense crowd of soldiers and some civilians. Besides the dead, he wounded 39 others. He may well be disturbed, but he also clearly acted out what Islamic jihad theology calls upon all Muslims to do. Hasan had long said openly he was a faithful Muslim. And in Hasan's own words, a faithful Muslim puts his faith ahead of his country. (Fundamentalists in the Christian faith sometimes say the same thing.) Recall that Islamic theology regards the secular nation-state as a corruption of God's law. Christianity does not. ("Render unto Caesar what is Caesar's and unto God what is God's" according to Jesus, as quoted in the New Testament.)

As for divided loyalty, recall that Robert E. Lee, who had taken a vow to support the United States upon graduating from West Point and had served it faithfully for his whole career, still felt an even greater loyalty to his own state of Virginia when the Civil War broke out. Conflicted for some weeks, Lee finally opted for Virginia despite being offered command of the Union army by General Winfield Scott. Still Robert E. Lee stuck by the slave state of Virginia. No one claimed Lee was nuts. Many other Union officers made the same choice to serve their states, not the Union. Lee and the others may have made a big mistake but that is not the same thing as being nuts.

Clearly Hasan had long been torn between duty to country (which after all paid for his college and medical school education) and his duty to Allah. Clearly Hasan resolved the conflict by coming down on the side of Allah. (Who knows but what the prospect of 70-odd nubile virgins tipped the scale for Hasan, who was still single. After all, were he to die in Allah's jihad against the infidels, those virgins are the promised reward according to established Islamic theology.)

Now the above remark is off the charts in terms of its political incorrectness. That is why I made it. The virgins-in-paradise reward is a real motivator in Islam in part because of the constraints that Muslim culture places upon women. It becomes difficult for men to take advantage of women or even to get to know them, and that was part of the point. So it is a bit like the promise of heavenly milk and honey to the semi-starving. Western males, of course, are not so constrained by their culture regarding access to women. Islam's promise to men of free access to virgins in paradise seems blasphemous, not to mention obscene to Westerners. It is as if God conceived paradise as an open brothel. Thus, in polite and politically correct circles, one simply does not mention this feature of the Islamic faith, lest the faithful be offended.

Political correctness, in other words, could be considered an unindicted co-conspirator in the deaths of the 13 victims at Fort Hood, just as it might be in contributing to the formation and later collapse of the subprime mortgage bubble. PC ideology favors diversity, inclusiveness, and strongly believes all cultures are equal. PC discourages diverse views, however, and tends deliberately to obscure who the true enemies of the United States are. That surely inhibits our military in dealing with those enemies. Now why would Americans want to do that to themselves?

To answer that question we need to see why political correctness came to be.

The ideology of political correctness aimed to redress the long-standing, overt racism of America's Anglo Saxon cultural founders. Never mind that a similar strain of racism was endemic to Europe in general and that different versions were part of the culture in both China and Japan. The fact is, the English colonists (and later, American citizens) came close to destroying the many indigenous Amerindian cultures as they took over their land. (Spanish and Portuguese colonists, of course, did the same south of the Rio Grande.) Moreover, America's Southern states practiced slavery on the largest scale in the world until the mid-nineteenth century. Hundreds of thousands of black Africans died in horrible conditions in the slave ships that brought them to America. (Never mind the fact that black Africans themselves organized and promoted the slave markets. They captured and sold other blacks to Islamic slave traders long before America was even colonized. Also never mind that it was Britain's Royal Navy that stopped the slave trade cold once it was outlawed by Parliament and the American Congress early in the nineteenth century.)

All the above is a matter of historical record and hardly constitutes a proud past for the United States. Political correctness wants us to wallow in guilt over this past. If it stopped there and recognized the progress America has made since, confessing guilt would be good for our cultural soul. But it does not stop there. Political correctness generally dismisses progress. Still, that progress began when Lincoln decided to fight the South rather than give in when the slave states withdrew from the Union in April 1861. Progress continued with the Constitutional amendments that outlawed slavery. After a pause of a hundred years, a whole series of civil rights laws were enacted in the twentieth century almost entirely by white men of predominantly Anglo Saxon heritage.

Recall, the Civil War remains today by far the most costly war that America has ever fought. About 600,000 whites from both sides died to free about 3.5 million black slaves. (That is more dead than in all our other wars combined.) In short, for every six black slaves freed, one white soldier died. (To point out this fact, or to point out that some blacks sold other blacks into slavery to start the slave trade, is thought to be a most politically incorrect attempt to reduce white or American guilt. Nor is it well received to point to the large number of blacks who have gained high office since 1964 by election and appointment.)

Political correctness also ignores the fact that the 1964 civil rights laws that attempted to bring women into equality with men, and to end a multitude of discriminations based on race, ethnic identity, or religion were passed by an overwhelmingly white male Congress.

In short, politically correct ideology is itself an outstanding example of bias on the basis of race, ethnicity, and gender. It is in essence anti-American, anti-Christian, and anti-male. It also poses a great danger to the United States in our conflict with Islamic terrorism. Political correctness is doing everything it can to neutralize our defenses against our enemies, in this case Islamic true-believing fundamentalists, by denying they control Islam's theology and aim to destroy us if they can via jihad, violence, and terrorism because, in their view, we stand as an obstacle to the success of their vision of pan-Islamic world peace and brotherhood.

The Hasan incident raises another issue, one that admittedly is politically incorrect to bring up. That is the potential among American Muslims such as Hasan for divided loyalty between their faith and their country. Now Hasan is native-born and his family insists he was raised as a good American. Still, his faith commanded him to choose his faith over his country and that is exactly what he did. And he made that choice after taking the vows of loyalty required of every American officer, and despite the benefits his country had given him. That same scriptural command is there for all Muslims. That is far from saying all Muslims are prepared to follow that command. But the question still remains, how is one to tell?

The problem with the Islamic faith for American citizens is this. The United States expects its citizens to support the Constitution and to be loyal to their country first and above all. A good Muslim cannot do that and at the same time be faithful to Islam. The reason is that a truly faithful Muslim will follow the path of jihad (if not personally, then in support of those who do). Jihad in turn, quite openly works toward the goal, by violent means where necessary, of getting rid of all nation-states in favor of one huge Islamic brotherhood run by a kind of theocracy that would be anathema to our Constitution. In fact it is anathema for almost precisely the same reasons that communism was. Communism, too, put faith in the ideology ahead not only of the state, but of the family, clans, and tribes. They advocated a violent overthrow of the government to achieve their goal. For that reason we officially made membership in the communist party semi-illegal. Some American communists, in fact, proved to be traitors, although not all or even most of them were. Islam, however, has a big advantage in that it gets the legal protections of a religion, even being exempt from taxes. Yet, in terms of its theology, Islam is not so much a religion as political theocracy. As such it openly disavows nearly all the provisions of our Constitution and supports its "overthrow by force if necessary." So what are we Americans going to do about that? So far, thanks to PC, we have simply refused to face facts. But here let me ask an obvious question. We do not give tax exemption to ideologies that promote a political agenda. Why should we make Islam an exception?

This brings us back to the issue of making the United States independent of Islamic oil. As of now, we are heavily dependent on it. Even nations that we regard as allies, such as Saudi Arabia, Kuwait, and the other gulf kingdoms such a Qatar and Dubai, cannot be depended upon to remain friendly. Recall that it was an embargo on shipments of oil to the United States by Saudi Arabia that triggered the OPEC oil price crisis in 1973. We were also once very friendly with Iran, remember, and even, to some extent, with Iraq. Meanwhile, much of the oil produced in the former Soviet Union is in the hands of Muslim states.

We can never preclude surprises in the future; by their very nature we cannot reliably plan for them. We have to deal with them as they come, but we do that more efficiently the more flexible are the economic institutions we create. The military has long lived by the doctrine of mobility and of having mobile reserves to deal with surprise attacks. The fall of France in 1940 stands as mute testimony. France had a rigid, fixed-in-place Maginot Line. That Line was virtually unbreakable. But when the Germans struck with massed armor around the flank from an unexpected direction, the French army collapsed even though they had a better tank (the Char B) and just as many soldiers, because they had no mobile reserves to block the German advance. When the Germans struck again on that same flank in December of 1944, America's master of mobility, General George Patton, shocked everyone, including his boss, General Eisenhower, with the speed and effectiveness of his response, which stopped the Germans cold.

This principle has wide applicability, particularly in economics. We were crippled after the market collapse in 1929 because we had a labor force built around the rigidities of hired labor. On a lesser scale our rigidities hurt us again during the OPEC oil price crises of 1973–75 and 1979–82. They hurt us even more after 1978 as Japan's competition in the automobile and electronics industries dug deeply into our markets. Classical economists argued that a hired labor force is needed to provide mobility. Workers that could be fired when not needed in one industry would be free to shift to other industries. True enough, but hired workers are much more defensive about their jobs. Wherever they work, they also resist working outside their designated job. Such job defensiveness much retards the adoption of better machinery, methods, and processes. That, in turn, leads to the retention of obsolete jobs to avoid the trauma of layoffs. Also, some managers fear that trauma may lead to retaliation by laid-off workers who, in their despair, may decide to "go postal." Japanese firms proved much faster at adopting new technology in their mature corporations because the workers did not fear being laid off as the result of better methods or technology. Thus, by 1980 Toyota was vastly more efficient at making automobiles than was General Motors. General Motors could lay off workers to be sure, but that sort of mobility did not solve their problem; the layoffs made it worse.

As for freeing ourselves from dependence on Islamic oil, much will depend on the future of energy technology. And yet, we cannot really plan on what the future of that technology will be. Before any such new technology is up and running, we need to create a truly flexible labor force. That can happen mainly by encouraging capital and labor to join in partnership. The inherent unit labor cost flexibility of partnership will let our companies respond more flexibly to surprises and make adjustments as they are needed. From about 1956 to 1978, while mesmerized by the mainframe computers and their supposed ability to forecast the future, managers placed their hopes in planning, a la Robert McNamara. Planning failed miserably when it came to surprises such as the OPEC oil price shocks. Operations managers learned that lesson the hard way. They learned that, in the real world of chaotic turbulence, we cannot accurately predict the future. As a matter of principle, turbulence makes accurate forecasts impossible. We thus live with a sort of macro version of Heisenberg's subatomic uncertainty principle.

Sad to say, the financial sector did not get that message. They continued to believe that they could use mainframe computers and clever algorithms to predict the future in a way to allow them to control risk. Having "controlled" risk, they launched into highly leveraged speculations, eager to get rich quick. So sure were they that they could control risk, that many convinced themselves that, in their greed, they were doing God's work of wealth creation. The crash of 2008 proved them wrong. Unfortunately, it is not yet clear they understand.

NOTE

1. Quoted in Efraim Karsh's *Islamic Imperialism: A History.* New Haven: Yale, 2006, p. 214, my italics.

BIBLIOGRAPHY

Armstrong, Karen. *A History of God: The 4,000-Year Quest of Judaism, Christianity, and Islam*. New York: Ballantine Books, 1993.

————. *Islam: A Short History*. New York: Random House, 2000.

Baker, Dean. *Plunder and Blunder: The Rise and Fall of the Bubble Economy*. Sausalito, CA: PoliPoint Press, 2009.

Behe, Michael. *Darwin's Black Box: The Biochemical Challenge to Evolution*. New York: The Free Press, 1996.

Behravesh, Nariman. *Spin-Free Economics: A No-Nonsense, Nonpartisan Guide to Today's Global Economic Debates*. New York: McGraw-Hill, 2009.

Bradley, James. *Flyboys: A True Story of Courage*. Boston: Little Brown & Co., 2004.

Capra, Fritjof. *The Web of Life: A New Scientific Understanding of Living Systems*. New York: Anchor Books, 1996.

Cohan, William D. *House of Cards: A Tale of Hubris and Wretched Excess on Wall Street*. New York: DoubleDay, 2009.

Collins, Jim. *How the Mighty Fall: And Why Some Companies Never Give In*. New York: HarperCollins, 2008.

D'Este, Carlo. *Warlord: A Life of Winston Churchill at War 1874–1945*. New York: HarperCollins, 2008.

Diamond, Jared. *Collapse: How Societies Choose to Fail or Succeed*. New York: Viking-Penguin, 2005.

————. *Guns, Germs, and Steel: The Fates of Human Societies*. New York: Norton, 1999.

Ehrlich, Paul. *Human Nature: Genes, Culture, and the Human Prospect*. Harmondsworth, UK: Penguin, 2004.

Elliott, Larry and Dan Atkinson. *The Gods That Failed: How Blind Faith in Markets Has Cost Us Our Future*. Nation Books: New York, 2009.

Faber, David. *And the Roof Caved In: How Wall Street's Greed and Stupidity Brought Capitalism to Its Knees*. Hoboken, NJ: John Wiley & Sons, 2009.

Ferguson, Niall. *The Ascent of Money: A Financial History of the World*. New York: Penguin Press, 2008.

Freeman, Charles. *Egypt, Greece, and Rome: Civilization in the Ancient Mediterranean*. Oxford: Oxford University Press, 1996.

Friedman, Thomas J. *The Lexus and the Olive Tree*. New York: Farrar, Straus and Giroux, 1999.

————. The *World Is Flat: A Brief History of the Twenty-First Century*. [rev. ed.] New York: Picador, 2007, c2005.

Galbraith, John Kenneth. *The Affluent Society*. Boston: Houghton Mifflin, 1956.

Gleick, James. *Chaos: The Making of a New Science*. New York: Viking, 1997.

Goldberg, Jonah. *Liberal Fascism: The Secret History of the American Left, from Mussolini to the Politics of Meaning*. New York: Broadway Books, 2009, c2007.

Grant, Michael. *The History of Rome*. New York: Scribner's, 1978.

Hauser, Marc. *The Evolution of Communication*. Cambridge, MA: MIT Press, 1996.

Hilton, Isabel. "The Pashtun Code." *New Yorker*, December 3, 2003, 59–72.

Huntington, Samuel P. *The Clash of Civilizations and the Remaking of the World Order*. New York: Simon and Schuster, 1996.

Karsh, Efraim. *Islamic Imperialism: A History*. New Haven, CT: Yale University Press, 2006.

Keynes, John Maynard. *The General Theory of Employment Interest and Money*. New York: McMillan, 1936.

Kuhn, Thomas. *The Structure of Scientific Revolutions*. Chicago: University of Chicago Press, 1962.

Lewis, Bernard. *The Crisis of Islam: Holy War and Unholy Terror*. New York: Random House, 2003.

Lewis, Michael, ed. *Panic: The Story of Financial Insanity*. New York: Norton, 2009.

Lockyer, Bill. quoted in *The Palm Springs (CA) Desert Sun*, October 26, 2009.

Mackay, Charles. *Extraordinary Popular Delusions and the Madness of Crowds*. 1841. Reprint, Radford, VA: Wilder Publications, 2008.

McDonald, Lawrence G. *A Colossal Failure of Common Sense: The Inside Story of the Collapse of Lehman Brothers*. New York: Crown Publishers, 2009.

Morris, Charles. *The Two Trillion Dollar Meltdown*. New York: Public Affairs Books, 2009.

Myrdal, Gunnar. *Asian Drama*. New York: Penguin, 1968.

Phillips, Kevin. *Bad Money: Reckless Finance, Failed Politics and the Global Crisis of American Capitalism*. New York: Viking, 2008.

Smick, David. *The World Is Curved: Hidden Dangers of the Global Economy*. New York: Penguin, 2008.

Smith, Adam. *An Inquiry into the Nature and Causes of the Wealth of Nations*. London: Ward, Lock, & Bowden & Co., 1776.

Soros, George. *The Crash of 2008 and What It Means: The New Paradigm for Financial Management*. [rev. ed.] New York: Public Affairs, 2009, c2008.

Spencer, Robert. *Religion of Peace? Why Christianity Is and Islam Isn't*. Washington DC: Regnery, 2007.

Taylor, Frederick Winslow. *Principles of Scientific Management*. 1911. Reprint, New York: Norton Co., 1967.

Vanden Heuval, Katrina, ed. *Meltdown: How Greed and Corruption Shattered Our Financial System and How We Can Recover*. New York: Nation Books, 2009.

Wallace, William McDonald. "Cultural Values and Economic Development: A Case Study of Japan." Ph.D. diss., University of Washington, 1963.

————. "The Great Depression Reconsidered: Implications for Today." *Contemporary Economic Policy* 13 (April 1995): 1–15.

———. *Postmodern Management: The Coming Partnership between Employees and Stock-holders*. Westport, CT: Greenwood/Quorum, 1998.

———. *Techno-Cultural Evolution: Cycles of Creation and Conflict*. Dulles, VA: Potomac Books, 2006.

Weber, Max. *The Protestant Ethic and the Spirit of Capitalism*. Translated by Talcott Parsons. New York: Scribner's, 1958.

Wheatley, Margaret. *Leadership and the New Science: Discovering Order in a Chaotic World*. 2nd ed. San Francisco: Berrett Koehler, 1999.

INDEX

About the Author

WILLIAM MCDONALD WALLACE has an MBA and PhD from the University of Washington in Seattle, served as a management and economic consultant, mostly overseas for about 10 years, retired from Boeing as Chief Economist for commercial airplanes for 20 years until retiring in 1992. He then taught economics and business at Saint Martin's University until retiring in 2008. Wallace now lives with his wife Patricia in the Palm Springs area of California. He has a son, daughter, stepdaughter, and two grandchildren.